Critical praise for this book

'This is an important contribution to the current debate on the relationship between peace and international justice ... I enjoyed reading it and learnt much from it ... an excellent work.' – JUSTICE RICHARD GOLDSTONE, former Chief Prosecutor of the United Nations International Criminal Tribunals for the former Yugoslavia and Rwanda (The Hague Tribunal) and chairperson of the International Independent Inquiry on Kosovo.

'An important and revealing account of efforts to resolve a bitter, exploitative, and under reported conflict that the international community should, and could have ended many, many years ago. Tim Allen has provided an early insight into the problems of resortin~ ' International Criminal Court i~ stance. If the ICC car conflict with the lives children at its core, wh broadcaster

'Presents powerful and empirical support for the relevance of the ICC in one of the world's worst humanitarian disasters.' – DAVID KEEN, author of *Conflict and Collusion in Sierra Leone* and *The Benefits of Famine*

'Trial Justice is a timely and important contribution to a critical – and often contentious – debate about the role of international criminal justice in times of war and peace.' – ERIC STOVER, author of *The Witnesses: War Crimes and the Promise of Justice in The Hague*, and Director of the Human Rights Center and Adjunct Professor, School of Public Health, University of California, Berkeley

Critical praise for this book

'Tim Allen has written a gripping and affirmative account of the complex encounter between international criminal law and African realities.' – MARY KALDOR, author of *New and Old Wars: Organized Violence in a Global Era*, and Director of the Centre for the Study of Global Governance

'A seminal work that carefully evaluates the conflict that has raged in the region for nearly twenty years. Allen is an anthropologist ... who has been working in Northern Uganda for some time. His work, therefore, is of significant value. He is one of a handful of authors ... whose writing is supported by a deep knowledge and clear understanding of both the social complexities and the political realities of the region.' – JOANNA QUINN, Assistant Professor of Political Science, University of Western Ontario, commenting on a draft of the book in *Transitional Justice Forum* (http://tj-forum.org/archives/001506.html)

'Tim Allen has written a provocative and illuminating analysis of the emerging practice of a new and potentially significant player in international affairs: the ICC.' – JENNY KUPER, author of *International Law Concerning Child Civilians in Armed Conflict* and *Military Training and Children: Law, Policy and Practice*

About the author

Dr Tim Allen is Reader in Development Studies at the London School of Economics. He has carried out long-term field research in Sudan and Uganda, and has also researched in other African countries, including Botswana, Ghana, Kenya and Zimbabwe. He has written extensively on issues of healing and suffering in Africa, on war-damaged populations, on aid programmes and on wider issues of international development. His publications include the bestselling textbook, *Poverty and Development* (edited with Alan Thomas, OUP), *Divided Europeans* (edited with John Eade, Kluwer), *The Media of Conflict* (edited with Jean Seaton, Zed Books), *Culture and Global Change* (edited with Tracey Skelton, Routledge), and two books on the repatriation and homecoming of African refugees.

His most recent work includes articles on HIV/AIDS policies in Uganda and Botswana. He is also a broadcaster and has presented or contributed to numerous radio programmes for the Open University and the BBC, including a series of eight programmes about Uganda for the World Service (broadcast in 2002). In 2001 he was elected to the Academy of Social Sciences for contributions in the application of anthropology to development issues.

TIM ALLEN

Trial justice

The International Criminal Court
and the Lord's Resistance Army

Zed Books
LONDON | NEW YORK

in association with

International African
Institute

 davidphilip

Trial justice: the International Criminal Court and the Lord's Resistance Army was first published in 2006 by

in Southern Africa: David Philip (an imprint of New Africa Books)
99 Garfield Road, Claremont 7700, South Africa

in the rest of the world: Zed Books Ltd, 7 Cynthia Street, London N1
9JF, UK and Room 400, 175 Fifth Avenue, New York, NY 10010, USA
<www.zedbooks.co.uk>

in association with the International African Institute, SOAS,
Thornhaugh Street, Russell Square, London WC1H 0XG, UK
<www.iaionthe.net>

Cover designed by Andrew Corbett
Set in Arnhem and Futura Bold by Ewan Smith, London
index: <ed.emery@britishlibrary.net>
Printed and bound in the UK by Biddles Ltd

Distributed in the USA exclusively by Palgrave Macmillan, a division
of St Martin's Press, LLC, 175 Fifth Avenue, New York, NY 10010.

A catalogue record for this book is available from the British Library
US CIP data are available from the Library of Congress

ISBN 978 1 84277 736 7 hb
ISBN 978 1 84277 737 4 pb

Contents

Illustrations

Acronyms

ACCORD	A series of publications from Conciliation Resources reviewing peace initiatives
ACORD	Agency for Cooperation and Research in Development
ARLPI	Acholi Religious Leaders' Peace Initiative
AVSI	Associazione Volontari per il Servizio Internazionale
CSOPNU	Civil Society Organization for Peace in Northern Uganda
DFID	Department for International Development (the UK's aid ministry)
EDF	Equatoria Defence Force (a militia group in Sudan)
FRONASA	Front for National Salvation (a military force led by President Museveni, which collaborated with the UNLA in the overthrow of Amin)
HSMF	Holy Spirit Mobile Forces
ICC	International Criminal Court
ICJ	International Court of Justice
ICTR	International Criminal Tribunal for Rwanda
ICTY	International Criminal Tribunal for Yugoslavia
IMF	International Monetary Fund
LC	Local council (these are councils introduced by President Museveni's government. They used to be called Resistance Councils. There are councils at each level of administration, from the village – LC1 – to the district – LC5)
LRA	Lord's Resistance Army
MSF	Médécins sans Frontières
NRA	National Resistance Army (the former name of the Ugandan army after President Museveni seized power)
OAU	Organization of African Unity
OTP	Office of the Chief Prosecutor of the ICC (also appears as ICC-OTP)
RPF	Rwandan Patriotic Front
SCiU	Save the Children in Uganda
SCSL	Special Court for Sierra Leone

SPLA	Sudan People's Liberation Army
UNHCR	United Nations High Commissioner for Refugees
UNICEF	United Nations Children's Fund
UNLA	Uganda National Liberation Army (the name of the Ugandan army after the overthrow of Idi Amin)
UPA	Uganda People's Army (a rebel group operating in Teso region in the 1990s)
UPDA	Uganda People's Democratic Army (a rebel force, largely made up of former UNLA soldiers)
UPDF	Uganda People's Defence Force (the new name of the Ugandan army)
WFP	World Food Programme
WHO	World Health Organization

Preface

Northern Uganda is the site of one of the worst humanitarian disasters in the world. Over a million people live in atrocious conditions in more than 200 displacement camps. It has been like this for years, but until recently it has been largely ignored. There have been the occasional news stories about weird cults, healing rituals, abducted children and mutilated women, but little serious effort to engage with the issues, or even to recognize the scale of the problem. During the past year there have been signs that things might finally be about to change. One reason for this is the role being played by the recently created International Criminal Court (ICC). It has intervened during an ongoing war, with a mandate to end impunity for the worst of crimes. The underlying assumption is that targeted criminal justice will contribute to peacemaking. It is an experiment that has caused a storm of controversy. The following chapters assess these developments and place them in the context of international criminal law and the local political circumstances in which they have occurred.

For me, the borderlands of Uganda and Sudan carry a special significance. This is where I went to live over twenty years ago, initially as a teacher in rural secondary schools and at Juba University, and later as a field researcher among the Acholi and Madi people. Altogether I spent four years in southern Sudan and two years in northern Uganda. Returning to the region in late 2004 for the first time in over a decade was a very moving experience. I met people whom I had not seen since they were small children and old friends who had a great deal to tell me. I also visited the graves of some of those I lived with, and was filled with sadness at how little improvement had been possible for most families. So much effort had been invested in earning small amounts of money and trying to educate their children. Yet there is so little to show for it. Indeed, for so many the situation is far worse than anything I saw in the 1980s.

Research in northern Uganda was carried out for three weeks during November 2004, for two weeks in March 2005, and at various times while I was living with my family in northern Uganda between May and September. The manuscript was completed in August, before the ICC issued warrants. A further visit was made to the region in November 2005, and a postscript has been added to the book drawing on findings from that trip, and bringing events up to date. By the time the book is published it is possible that one or more of the Lord's Resistance Army commanders will have been taken to The Hague for trial. One of them at least is worried about that prospect, and has been using his access to a satellite telephone to solicit legal advice.

Most of the research in November 2004 and March 2005 took place in Gulu, Kitgum, Lira, Adjumani and Pader municipalities, and in displacement camps at Awee, Opit, Awere, Lalogi, Anaka, Labuje, Pader, Pagimo, Corner Ogur, Abia, Agweng, Atiak and Pabbo. Numerous group meetings were held with local council officers, NGO staff, soldiers etc. But an effort was also made to spend time with individuals and solicit their views in private. Interviews and discussions were held in English, in Lwo (the language of the Acholi and Langi people), and in Maditi (the language spoken by Madi people of Adjumani district). When visiting the camps for the internally displaced, I tried to spend nights there rather than return to Gulu or Kitgum. This was not something that research teams had usually done, which may help explain the differences in local views presented here from those in other reports and articles. I made almost all the interviews in November 2004 and March 2005 with one or other of my two research assistants, Jackie Atigo and Tonny Odiya Labol. Unless otherwise noted, those quoted in the report took place in the Lwo language. During the period between May and September 2005 I was running a research project on the return of 'formerly abducted people' to their families, involving quite a large research team. This made it possible to visit many more camps. Visits were made by the team to most of the larger camps and a large number of the smaller ones too. Around four hundred interviews were made with individuals and groups, including district officials, aid agency staff, peace negotiators, military officers, LRA combatants and over two hundred people living in the camps. Visits were also made to The Hague in 2005 for discussions with staff at the ICC. In addition to this recent research, the book draws extensively on my earlier long-term fieldwork in northern Uganda and across the border in Sudan from the early 1980s until 1991, and on the many reports, articles, books and dissertations dealing with the area.

To carry out field research in the war zone of northern Uganda is not straightforward. It is easy enough to spend time in the main towns and some of the more accessible camps, but to reach the places where most people live requires transport and logistical support. I am very grateful to the aid agencies that assisted in the research. I have not named them because some of the arguments made in the book deal with sensitive issues, and do not necessarily represent their views. Much of the funding for the fieldwork and writing up was paid for by the Crisis States Research Centre of the London School of Economics (LSE), which is supported by the UK's Department of International Development.

Several perceptive and rigorous commentators have responded to drafts of the book, and provided me with help and suggestions, including Barney Afako, Erin Baines, Betty Bigombe, Adam Branch, Matthew Brubacher, Christin Chinkin, Filippo Ciantia, Chis Dolan, Sverker Finnstrom, Susanne Kirk, Elliott Green,

Mariana Goetz, Matt Hobson, Tania Kaiser, Susanne Kirk, Jenny Kuper, Bob Leitch, Zachary Lomo, Andy Mawson, Ben Mergelsberg, Dyan Mazurana, Adam O'Brian, Gabriel Oling Olang, Melissa Parker, James Putzel, Joanna Quinn, Mareike Schomerus, Eric Stover, David Wright and others whom I cannot name. It must be stressed, however, that the analysis presented here does not necessarily represent the views of any of these people. In fact some of them strongly disagree with what I have written.

I was diagnosed with acute myeloid leukaemia five years ago. I am grateful beyond measure to my anonymous bone marrow donor and to haematology staff at University College Hospital, London, for saving my life. The support received from colleagues at the LSE, my parents, friends and relatives has also been invaluable, and I would not have been able to return to Africa and carry out this research without it. Finally, I thank Luke, Joshua and Rachael for putting up with me while I wrote the book, and above all Melissa for her constant love and care.

for Melissa

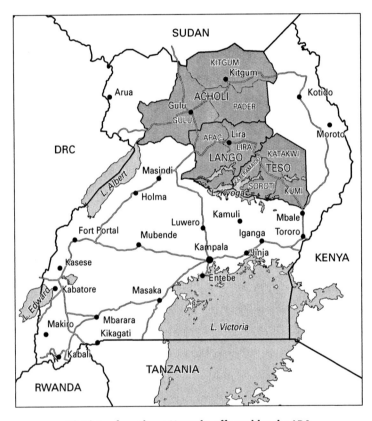

Districts of northern Uganda affected by the LRA

IDP populations receiving relief assistance, based on OCHA estimates

Total IDP population (April/July 2005): approximately 1.5 million living in over 250 IDP camps (excluding unregistered IDPs)

Breakdown by district

Districts with a predominantly Acholi population

Gulu district: total IDP population (July 2005) 460,226 living in 53 IDP camps

Kitgum district: total IDP population (July 2005) 310,111 living in 22 IDP camps

Pader district: total IDP population (April 2005) 283,781 living in 26 IDP camps

Districts with a predominantly Langi population

Apac district: total IDP population (July 2005) 98,193 living in 15 IDP camps

Lira district: total IDP population (July 2005) 350,828 living in 40 IDP camps

Districts with a predominantly Teso population

Katakwi district: total IDP population (April 2005) approximately 140,000 living in 82 IDP camps

Soroti, Kaberamaido and Kumi districts: total IDP population (July 2005) 18,000 living in 22 IDP camps

(*Source*: OCHA, 2005)

1 | Introduction: ending impunity

In December 2003 President Yoweri Museveni of Uganda asked the prosecutor of the International Criminal Court (ICC) to investigate 'the situation concerning the Lord's Resistance Army'.[1] The LRA have been waging war in the north of the country since the mid-1980s. Most of those caught up in the conflict have been from the Acholi population of Gulu, Kitgum and Pader districts, but neighbouring areas of Lira, Apac, Adjumani, Kumi and Soroti districts, where the people are predominantly Langi, Madi and Teso, have also been affected. Abductions, including the kidnapping of children, have been common, and hundreds of people had been compelled to kill and maim or be killed and maimed themselves. Victims have had lips, hands and fingers cut off. Some have been forced to slaughter their own parents, or drink the blood of those they have murdered. Several massacres of civilians have occurred, and hundreds of thousands of people are living in displacement camps, where conditions are often appalling. The scale of suffering is immense, and there is no doubt that crimes have been perpetrated that fall within the jurisdiction of the court.

The ICC is a new institution, and the legal process in northern Uganda was to be its first big case. The decision to establish it had been taken in July 1998, when 121 of the 148 states represented at a conference in Rome agreed to accept the text of the proposed statute. The vote followed five weeks of intense and sometimes acrimonious discussion, and many years of lobbying by humanitarian agencies and human rights activists.

Inevitably, the statute is full of compromises and several parts of it show signs of haste. The awkward mixed metaphor at the

1

start of the preamble is just one of many examples. It tells us that 'all peoples are united by common bonds, their cultures pieced together in a shared heritage', and expresses concern that 'this delicate mosaic may be shattered at any time'.[2] But other parts of the document move beyond empty rhetoric, and make clear and unequivocal statements. In so doing they assert a commitment to invigorate international law and move it in a new direction. States signing the Rome Treaty affirmed 'that the most serious crimes of concern to the international community as a whole must not go unpunished and that their effective prosecution must be ensured by taking measures at the national level and by enhancing international cooperation'. They were determined 'to put an end to impunity for the perpetrators of those crimes', and were resolved 'to guarantee lasting respect for the enforcement of international justice'. Much to the surprise of sceptics, who thought this was just one more example of end-of-millennium wishful thinking, the sixty ratifications of the Rome Treaty that were needed to bring the statute into force were accumulated within four years. As a consequence the jurisdiction of the ICC came into effect on 1 July 2002.

Quite what this means in practice is yet to be established. The implications of setting up the court may be far reaching, or its role may be circumscribed by US antipathy and the reluctance of those states that have ratified the Rome Statute (i.e. 'State Parties') to act effectively on its behalf. Perhaps not surprisingly, the waters are being tested in parts of the world that are politically and economically of limited significance for the major powers. All the ICC's ongoing investigations are in central Africa.[3] The referral by the government of Uganda was followed by state party referrals from the governments of the Democratic Republic of the Congo in April 2004[4] and the Central African Republic in January 2005. Then, in March 2005, alleged crimes committed in the Darfur region of Sudan were referred by the UN Security

**1 The massacre at Pagak in Gulu district, May 2004
(anonymous)**

Council. This new case is hugely significant for the ICC, but at the time of writing in mid-2005 the investigation and preparation of warrants are at a relatively early stage. Up to now, the Ugandan case has been the most important, and also the most controversial.

That atrocities have happened in northern Uganda is well established, even if the war between the Ugandan government and the LRA has rarely been covered in the international media. Indeed, the United Nations Children's Fund (UNICEF) had suggested that events in Uganda would be an ideal case for the ICC back in 1998. In the months immediately after the referral, further gruesome killings occurred, including one of the worst individual incidents of the war when some two hundred unarmed people were massacred at Barlonya camp on 21 February 2004.[5] Photographs taken the morning after another incident at Pagak in May show the bodies of women and children. They are lying,

Introduction

3

quite neatly, in the grass next to each other where they were killed. Each has its skull smashed, including the babies, who are still wrapped in their shawls on their mothers' backs.

Expectations that such events would lead to relatively straightforward prosecutions and convictions were, however, soon found to be misplaced. The complexities on the ground clearly took the ICC by surprise. It has found itself on a steep learning curve, dealing with intense local as well as international opposition. Fundamental issues have been raised about what justice means in an African war zone and about how political order can be established. Among other things, a commitment to ending impunity sets limits to what can be offered in peace agreements. In August 2005, a year after the Office of the Prosecutor began formal investigations, warrants have been prepared but not publicly issued (NB: it subsequently became known that sealed warrants had been issued in July 2005 – see Postscript). The court has had to bide its time, waiting for the right moment – and for key donors to give the go-ahead for it to act. Nevertheless, the capacities and status of the ICC have been rising. It has become a key factor in the ongoing negotiations, and has positioned itself to have a pivotal role both here and north of the border in Sudan.

This book is about what happened when international criminal justice was introduced to northern Uganda. It interrogates myths and misunderstandings, and explains why the ICC intervention has not proceeded as initially planned. It also shows why recent developments in Uganda may have far-reaching effects. But first, it is necessary to provide some background information about developments in international criminal justice.

International law and the most serious crimes

For some political analysts, international law does not really exist. The term is commonly used to refer to a body of rules laid out in agreements between states.[6] These rules have a rhetorical significance in diplomacy, but they are not impartially applied and may at times be ignored by a government if they are not considered to be in the 'national interest'. The rules suggest that states are bound to behave in appropriate ways, but where is the mechanism for ensuring that this happens? Responses to the absence of sanctions have involved trying to hold the governments of states to account by making it apparent that it is in their interests to regulate their own actions and to make them feel uncomfortable if they do not. There are in fact a large number of regulations that are widely observed, at least partly because they are essential for the economies of the richest and most powerful states, which collectively exert pressure on weaker states to comply. Such regulations make, for example, international investments, trade and air travel possible. But in other areas, persuasion has been less effective. For example, controls on environmental degradation have been resisted and all kinds of human rights have been set aside at will. With respect to the latter, Amnesty International has persistently drawn the attention of governments to failures in their apparent obligations under conventions their states have signed and ratified. It can have an effect in some circumstances, but the worst offenders generally do not care much about what Amnesty International or any other well-meaning group has to say.

The possibility that international law might offer more than a set of 'best practice' codes of conduct for governments, and also the reality that it often does not, is closely connected with agreements reached at the end of the Second World War. Still shaken by events, including the recent liberation of the Nazi death camps, the founders of the UN system had wanted to ensure that such things could not happen again. According to its charter, the 'Peoples of the United Nations' were determined 'to save succeeding generations from the scourge of war', 'to reaffirm faith in fundamental human rights' and 'to establish

5

conditions under which justice and respect for the obligations arising from treaties and other sources of international law can be maintained'. In a series of articles grouped in Chapter VII of the charter, the Security Council was mandated with the task of taking action 'with respect to threats to the peace, breaches of the peace, and acts of aggression'. Security Council resolutions were intended to be binding on all UN member states, and the council was given powers under Article 42 to take military action 'to maintain or restore international peace and security'.

At first it seemed that this new approach to international law, and particularly criminal justice, might have a chance of being made effective. A series of agreements outlined a radical clarification and extension of criminal accountability. In most respects, the Nuremberg Charter of August 1945 built on long-standing procedures for prosecuting captured enemies, but it made two very significant departures.[7] Article 6 referred to 'crimes against humanity' to describe 'persecution, enslavement, deportation and other inhumane acts' committed on a very large scale, and Article 7 rejected immunity, stating that 'the official position of defendants ... shall not be considered as freeing them from responsibility or mitigating punishment'. The proceedings that followed were not without their flaws. Systematic rape, for example, was ignored in the indictments, perhaps because it would have been difficult not to implicate the Soviet army. But the atrocious acts of those Nazi leaders found guilty were laid out in detail, their culpability established beyond question, and a model established for holding those most responsible for the worst crimes to account. Three years later, in 1948, came the Universal Declaration of Human Rights. It had no enforcement mechanisms and was not a statement of law, but it spelt out very clearly what an obligation to promote human rights means. It was also submitted for signature the day after the Convention on the Prevention and Punishment of the Crime of Genocide.

This did require states to prosecute and punish, either through domestic judicial procedures or 'by such international criminal tribunal as may have jurisdiction'.

These developments, together with the 1949 Geneva Conventions, promised a great deal, but there remained a crucial flaw. In the past there had been few international arrangements that sought to restrict the choices made by the governments of independent states, and concerns about possible infringements of sovereignty were reflected in Article 2 of the UN Charter. This precluded intervention 'in matters which are essentially within the domestic jurisdiction of the State'. Other articles of the charter reiterated the point, and respect for national sovereignty became a predominant aspect of post-Second World War international relations. To give just one important example, the International Court of Justice (ICJ) at The Hague was mandated to deal with any question of international law, but states have to refer cases themselves, and are free to choose not to do so (or even present a defence if they have opted out of that requirement).

The tension between international obligations and national sovereignty had been recognized in the UN Charter. Chapter VII was intended to deal with it in the more extreme cases. It quickly became apparent, however, that Chapter VII was inadequate. Permanent members of the Security Council could veto resolutions, and once divisions opened up between them, any agreement over enforcement measures became unlikely or impossible. By the time the Universal Declaration of Human Rights was signed, the cold war had begun in earnest. The Soviet ambassador to the UN dismissed it as 'just a collection of pious phrases'.[8] For the next forty years the superpowers themselves and their main allies repeatedly failed to comply with the post-Second World War agreements, and signed various others without any serious intention of being bound by them.[9] Appalling governments were supported and protected as long as they kept to the correct ideological

7

line. The list of puppet monsters that enjoyed impunity seems endless. Leaders like Kim Il Sung, Pol Pot, Mengistu, Pinochet, Mobutu and Barre acted without any expectation that they would ever be prosecuted for their barbaric behaviour.

The incapacity of the Security Council also meant that governments of newly independent countries could do just about anything they liked to domestic opponents under the guise of anti-colonialism. Non-interference and protection of borders inherited at independence became an obsession of the Organization of African Unity (OAU). Even the Tanzanian invasion of Uganda in 1971 to overthrow the dreadful regime of Idi Amin received no official support and was condemned as a breach of international law. Amin himself was allowed to live out his days in relative comfort in Saudi Arabia.

There were a few exceptions and glimmers of hope. The introduction of sanctions against apartheid South Africa by the UN in 1967, and their extension in 1977 as mandatory under Chapter VII of the UN Charter, indicated what could be done if there was enough political will. Also the founding of Amnesty International in 1961, as well as the emergence of other non-governmental organizations and human rights groups, revealed that the conventional dispensations of international diplomacy and power politics were not accepted by everyone, and might be resisted and opposed with a degree of success in some circumstances. Eventually the pressure on the US government over its activities in Vietnam proved overwhelming. But overall the human rights record was bleak and the idea of holding to account those individuals who committed crimes against humanity was manifestly a failure. It was not until the late 1980s that there was much prospect of this changing, when the ending of the cold war made it conceivable that the Security Council would take on the role that had initially been intended for it.

In the event, the 1990s did not witness the promised 'New

World Order'. On the contrary, it was a decade of humanitarian and human rights disasters, including the disintegration of Yugoslavia, the US-led intervention in Somalia, the genocide in Rwanda, the fall of Srebrenica, new wars in Liberia and Sierra Leone, ongoing wars in Sudan and Angola, and the disappearance of hundreds of thousands of people in Congo who were supposed to be under the protection of the Office of the United Nations High Commissioner for Refugees (UNHCR). Initially, the Security Council, led by the USA, took a highly interventionist approach, but by mid-decade confidence in militarized humanitarianism had waned. In 1994, at the insistence of the UK and the USA, the Security Council refused to accept that genocide was occurring in Rwanda, precisely because it would have meant that the 1948 Genocide Convention would apply and enforcement procedures be activated.

While ending the cold war did not lead to an era of peace and tranquillity, however, it did have the desirable effect of reducing incentives to cover up atrocities and keep mass murderers in power for strategic purposes. At the same time, the introduction of new techniques in television news coverage, such as 'real time' reporting and twenty-four-hour channels, combined with the publicity campaigns of human rights groups, fed demands among electorates in rich countries for something to be done. In this context, the Security Council decided to return to the precedent of Nuremberg and the notion of international criminal prosecution. Initially this was done in a distinctly half-hearted way, but it opened the door to some remarkable developments, including the creation of the ICC.

A resurgence of international criminal trials

In 1993 the Security Council set up the Hague Tribunal for War Crimes in Former Yugoslavia, otherwise known as the International Criminal Tribunal for the Former Yugoslavia (ICTY). It

9

did so by invoking Chapter VII of the UN Charter. Apparently the council had the power to hold perpetrators of the worst war crimes against humanity to justice after all. Indeed, an implication of Resolutions 808 and 827 is that the Security Council had always had an obligation to do so under its powers to keep the peace. Having done this for Yugoslavia, no case could be made for it not being done for Rwanda as well. The result was an appendage of the Hague Tribunal established in November 1994, known as the International Criminal Tribunal for Rwanda (ICTR).[10]

The fact that the Hague Tribunal was established as a subsidiary organ of the Security Council meant that all UN member states were obliged to cooperate with both the ICTY and the ICTR. So in theory they had considerable authority, not so unlike that of the Nuremberg Tribunal. There were, however, important contrasts with the situation in Europe in 1945. One of these was that the ICTY and ICTR could not impose the death penalty. Another was that indictments were not immediately followed by trials. The ICTY began to operate painfully slowly, while some of the worst events of the war in former Yugoslavia were occurring. These included the massacre at Srebrenica in July 1995, which was organized by Mladic and Karadzic, even though they had already been charged by the ICTY for their role in the bombardment of civilians in Sarejevo. In contrast, the ICTR was not established until six months after the mass killing of 1994 had stopped and many of those accused were to hand. Nevertheless, nothing seemed to happen with any urgency for several years.

The primary constraint for the ICTY was that the commanders of NATO forces were unwilling to put their troops at risk in order to secure arrests, and correctly interpreted the setting up of the tribunal as essentially a public relations exercise. The serious business of brokering peace agreements required negotiation and compromises with the leaders of warring factions. This had become accepted as the way to deal with armed conflict. Perpetrators of violence had to be given enough of what they wanted and protection from prosecution so that order could be restored, and despite the apparent weight of ICTY indictments in international law, in practice they were ignored. The first defendant, Dusko Tadic, was no more than a revolting thug who had fled to Germany, where he was recognized and arrested in Munich. He did not arrive in The Hague until 1995 and his trial did not begin for another year. It took yet another year for him to be sentenced, and two more years before the start of his appeal. Until 1998 there was no real prospect of the likes of Mladic or Karadzic, let alone Milosevic himself, being called to account.

In Arusha there were different difficulties.[11] In contrast to reactions to the ICTY there has been eagerness among those accused of crimes to be tried by the ICTR, partly because most of them were readily brought into custody and have wanted to avoid Rwandan justice procedures, but also because the prison life offered by the tribunal has its own attractions. An obscene situation developed in which those primarily responsible for the killing were living in relative comfort, while most of their surviving victims continued to live in poverty. In the early years there were also well-grounded allegations of corruption, and there have been very serious delays in legal processes, with some defendants having to wait for many years before their trials began. Logistical arrangements for setting up the tribunal infrastructure proved to be both daunting and very expensive. Hundreds of UN personnel and defence teams had to be supported in a location that lacks the facilities available in a city like The Hague. The UN system was not flexible enough to cope, and for a while staff had to accept three-month contracts, making it impossible to recruit the best candidates. Arusha is also not a place that is closely covered by the international media, so what has been happening there has been largely overlooked. Remarkably few trials have been concluded and both the Registry (which is responsible for organizational

One

issues) and Office of the Prosecutor have been open to charges of serious incompetence. The lack of adequate monitoring in Arusha suggests that here too international criminal justice was a means of seeming to do something, not a genuine effort by the governments of powerful states to reassert the principles agreed in the 1940s. The one really important conviction secured by the ICTY has been that of the former Rwandan prime minister, Jean Kambanda, who made things relatively easy by pleading guilty to the crime of genocide. That happened two months after the signing of the ICC Rome Statute in 1998 – an event that had perhaps helped focus proceedings.

To be fair, even without the administrative mess, the ICTR has been in an extremely awkward position. It has had to operate without the full cooperation of the Rwandan government, which has persistently viewed the ICTR as an imposition and sop to the guilt of the international community for its failures in 1994. The foreign base of the ICTR and the lack of a death penalty meant that the new Rwandan government had actually voted against the setting up of the tribunal in the Security Council (it was a non-permanent member of the council at the time). It has pointed out that justice procedures in Rwanda itself have not been adequately supported. The genocide had devastated the judiciary, and by 1996 there were over 100,000 people awaiting trial. In this situation the manoeuvrings in Arusha were dismissed as a scandalous waste of money. Instead, it was argued, resources would be better used supporting national and local procedures, including the new *gacaca* system, introduced in 2001/02 and expanded in 2003/04, based on 'traditional' mechanisms of conflict resolution, public exposition, compensation and forgiveness.[12]

Another problem has been that the ICTR can investigate only alleged crimes that have taken place in 1994. In particular, this means that it cannot deal with events after the Rwandan Patriotic Front (RPF) victory in the civil war, even though the new government has itself been implicated in mass killings, notably in eastern Congo in the late 1990s. It has made the ICTR appear to be biased. From 2002, the Hague Tribunal chief prosecutor, Carla Del Ponte, tried to do something about this by launching investigations of several senior RPF officers for crimes allegedly committed during 1994. Not surprisingly, it produced a furious reaction from the Rwandan government, and perhaps partly as a result, the Security Council decided in 2003 to create a separate prosecutor for the ICTR, thereby replacing Del Ponte. It made it unlikely that anyone from the RPF would ever be indicted, particularly given the growing impatience with the ICTR in the Security Council, and the pressure to quickly conclude prosecutions.

In contrast, more recent events at the ICTY have made it seem something of a success story. From 1998, again the year of the ICC's Rome Statute, NATO forces began to be more serious about arrests. At first it was middle-level figures, such as concentration camp commandants, but soon it was also generals, and even Karadzic's successor as Bosnian Serb president. Quite suddenly, more than half of those indicted were in custody. Then, in June 2001, Milosevic himself was handed over by Serbia, effectively in return for a large reconstruction grant. His trial began the following February. At first it did not seem to go well for the prosecution. Milosevic used the public platform to present his own political analysis, and he also proved very effective at undermining some of the prosecution's first witnesses. All this was watched with interest on television in former Yugoslavia, increasing his prestige in some quarters. But as time has passed he has been worn down and diminished. His reputation has gradually been taken apart by the relentless presentation of evidence.

Whatever the limitations of the ICTY and the ICTR, the creation of the Hague Tribunal did help clarify and crystallize various issues in international law during the 1990s, as well as extend its potential application. It reconnected it with the

13

idea of international criminal prosecution, something that had
been almost entirely ignored since the 1940s. It established that
international jurisdiction to punish both war crimes and crimes
against humanity applied to all states, whether or not they are
engaged in international armed conflict. It also reiterated that
individuals can be held to account for crimes against humanity,
war crimes or genocide under international law, and in the latter case secured pioneering convictions. Unlike Nuremberg, it
foregrounded rape as a war crime, and in addition established
it as a crime against humanity when committed systematically
and on a large scale. Perhaps most importantly of all, the ICTY
and ICTR provided experience of actually running international
criminal proceedings, something that had never actually been
done before if Nuremberg is discounted as an arrangement between four victorious allies. In so doing they suggested models
and principles that could be drawn upon in other situations.

One aspect of this has been applications of the concept of
'universal jurisdiction'. This holds that all national judicial systems have an obligation to investigate and adjudicate the most
grievous crimes, because they affect all humanity. The most spec-
tacular example was the arrest of General Pinochet in London in
October 1998.[13] Others include the indictment of Ariel Sharon in
Belgium by lawyers representing survivors of the Shatila and Sabra
massacres; the prosecution in Senegal of the former president
of Chad, Hissène Habré; and the prosecutions of Rwandans for
crimes perpetrated in their own country by a military tribunal in
Switzerland and by a civil court in Belgium. The Hague Tribunal
has also made internationally supported criminal justice mechanisms a serious prospect elsewhere too. Apart from being a factor
in the setting up of a permanent international court, it influenced
the emergence of new localized legal arrangements, such as the
agreement between the UN and the Cambodian government to
try some surviving Khmer Rouge leaders for atrocities perpetrated

in the 1970s, the setting up of a hybrid judicial system in Kosovo, and the creation of the Special Court for Sierra Leone (SCSL). The latter began to operate just a few months before the Rome Statute came into force, and has raised issues of relevance for the Ugandan intervention.

In 2000, Security Resolution 1315 recorded an arrangement between the UN and Sierra Leone to try those who bear the greatest responsibility for serious violations of international and Sierra Leonean law. Following several more months of continuous upheaval in the country, the court was finally established in January 2002 once British military intervention had imposed a degree of political stability. Like the ICTY and ICTR, the SCSL is an ad hoc response to a particular situation, linked to agreement in the Security Council, including support from the USA. But it differs from them in that it is a treaty-based court. In this respect it is similar to the ICC. Its rules of procedure follow those of the ICTR, but staff are a mixture of UN appointments and Sierra Leonean nationals, the majority of judges being appointed by the UN Secretary General. The hearings take place within Sierra Leone and the proceedings are, in effect, an extension of Sierra Leone's judiciary. This means that some of the difficulties that have arisen with the ICTR, and to a lesser extent the ICTY, might be avoided or ameliorated. It has not stopped the SCSL being locally controversial, but it more clearly aims at enhancing domestic legal processes through an international component, rather than laying down the law from a distance.

The fact that the SCSL is treaty based has, however, also proved to be a problem. The international criminal tribunals, as the creations of the Security Council, have considerable authority. No member state of the UN can legitimately refuse to recognize warrants – although, as we have seen, they may choose to ignore them in practice. This is less clear for the SCSL. In 2003, the SCSL indicted Charles Taylor, who was at the time still president of

Liberia. Liberia was not party to the treaty between Sierra Leone and the UN, and refused to recognize the warrant. To make matters worse, after Taylor left office he was given political asylum in Nigeria, which also refused to arrest him. Efforts were made to negotiate a solution, with the USA offering a reward of $2 million to anyone who would help remove Taylor to Sierra Leone to face trial. These developments have done nothing to enhance the Special Court's standing or the status of its warrants. It is a lesson that the ICC has not ignored.

The creation of the ICC

The decision to create a permanent international criminal tribunal or court dates back to the late 1940s. The wording of the Genocide Convention indicated that one would be established, and draft structures were prepared by the International Law Commission (ILC), the UN body responsible for codifying international law. But during the cold war these came to nothing. In the late 1980s President Gorbachev suggested resurrecting the idea as a means of dealing with terrorism, and interest was also expressed in the potential role of such a court in combating drug trafficking. It was the generally positive public reaction in rich countries to the setting up of the Hague Tribunal, however, which finally accelerated the process. The ILC was asked to come up quickly with a new proposal. This proved to be an exceedingly cautious affair, reflecting a continuing determination to resist any infringements on sovereignty. The ILC suggested setting up a court that would become involved in a case only if there was a referral from a state that was party to an international criminal law convention (such as the Genocide Convention) and had jurisdiction over the person accused of the relevant crime. In 1995, the UN General Assembly established a committee to seek views about the proposal and prepare a draft statute, but by that point there was a growing interest in something more ambitious.

The Rome Conference of 1998 was the last of a series of consultation meetings. It was supposed to agree a statute, ideally based on a consensus of all the participating states. There remained serious disagreements to resolve, however. Basically UN member states fell into three groups. One faction, mostly for obvious reasons, did not really want any sort of permanent international criminal court. It included Libya, Indonesia, Iran, Iraq and India. A second group wanted a court that could be activated only by the UN Security Council. It would therefore not be opposed by the USA and other permanent members, because they could be sure it would never act against their interests, and would be empowered, like the Hague Tribunal, under Chapter VII of the UN Charter. This was the kind of court wanted by the Clinton administration, as well as China and France. Ranged against these two groups were more than forty states and several hundred non-governmental agencies and associations. This group was far from homogeneous, but wanted a more powerful court, with an independent prosecutor unhindered by the Security Council. Canada and Germany were among those countries pushing for this kind of option, joined by the UK after the Labour Party came to power in 1997.

Several of those states wanting an independent court were keen to keep the USA on board. President Clinton had been vocal in support of an international criminal court, notably during his visit to Rwanda, so it was hoped that the USA would accept a majority view of what it should be like. In retrospect this was rather naive. Whatever the Clinton administration decided, it would have been very unlikely that Congress would have approved ratification for a very long time. It had, after all, taken the USA forty years to ratify the Genocide Convention, and there was fierce Republican opposition to overcome. In the event, on the final day of the conference the US delegation was still holding out for limitations on the powers of the court, particularly with respect to its jurisdiction over US peacekeeping forces. By this point in the proceedings the USA seems to have wanted the negotiations to break down, and so called for a vote on the existing draft. Its expectation may have been that other states would be unwilling to vote in favour of it without US support, and perhaps also without revising some of the more muddled, repetitive and redundant passages. They were wrong. Exasperated by US intransigence, only seven of the 148 participating states voted against it.

The statute of the International Criminal Court that emerged from the Rome Conference established a permanent and ostensibly independent institution, based at The Hague, with power to exercise jurisdiction over genocide, crimes against humanity, war crimes and, at some future date, the crime of aggression. It reiterates definitions of crimes in the various international criminal agreements adopted since the Genocide Convention, clarifies crimes against humanity, and confirms that war crimes may be committed during 'internal' or civil wars. It also emphasizes that individuals may be held to account, and that command responsibility is a basis for liability. A crime against humanity includes any of a list of crimes 'committed as part of a widespread or systematic attack directed against any civilian population, with knowledge of the attack'. Significantly for the situation in northern Uganda, the list includes murder; enslavement; deportation or forcible transfer of population; and sexual violence such as rape, sexual slavery and forced pregnancy. Confusingly these crimes are repeated in the lists of war crimes, sometimes with a change of wording. Among those war crimes listed in cases of 'armed conflict not of an international character' are mutilation; taking of hostages; extra-judicial executions; intentionally directing attacks against the civilian population; pillaging; conscripting or enlisting children under the age of fifteen; 'ordering the displacement of the civilian population for reasons related to the conflict, unless the security of the civilians involved or imperative military reasons so demand'; and the same sexual crimes as mentioned in the article relating to crimes against humanity.[14] Certain other issues are avoided altogether or sidestepped in the statute. The use of landmines and nuclear weapons are prime examples. Also, the failure of the Rome Conference to agree a definition of the crime of aggression was a serious disappointment. It was, after all, one of the main crimes that the UN system was set up to prevent.

As for the capacities of the court, the group of states and NGOs wanting a powerful and independent prosecutor achieved only a part of what they wanted, reflecting a desire to placate the USA. Significantly, Article 1 of the statute states that the court 'shall be complementary to national criminal jurisdictions', indicating that it does not have the kind of primacy of jurisdiction mandated to the ICTY and ICTR, but intervenes only when state parties are unable or unwilling to act. In a series of overlapping articles (13–16) it is explained that the exercise of the court's jurisdiction can begin in three ways. The prosecutor may initiate investigations on the basis of information on crimes within the jurisdiction of the court. If he or she concludes that there is a reasonable basis to proceed with an investigation, he or she can submit to the Pre-Trial Chamber a request for authorization. Alternatively, a state party (i.e. one of the states that have ratified the statute) can refer a situation to the court, or a situation may be referred to the prosecutor by the Security Council acting under Chapter VII of the UN Charter. It is also stipulated that no investigation or prosecution may be commenced or proceeded with for a period of twelve months after the Security Council has requested the court to that effect in a resolution adopted under Chapter VII. In addition, the statute states repeatedly that the court must act 'in the interests of victims' (Articles 53, 54, 65, 68) and 'in the interests of justice' (Articles 53, 55, 61, 65, 67), and provides generous provision for 'the rights of the accused' (e.g. Article 68).

All this means is that the ICC is potentially under the control of the Security Council, and to the extent that it is not under its control, the Office of the Prosecutor is constrained by the ICC judges in the Pre-Trial Chamber, by the requirement to work in conjunction with national judiciaries, and by a range of limitations on his or her power, potentially including extra-judicial considerations. As the ICC does not have its own police force, any investigation initiated by the prosecutor cannot proceed very far without the approval of the state involved. The prosecutor has to rely on the support of the state in order to carry out investigations on the ground and to arrest suspects if warrants are served. It is unlikely that a state that is not party to the ICC would be willing to do this, unless there is a Security Council resolution. Also, those states that are party to the ICC are not likely to be ruled by governments perpetrating acts that they think will fall under the jurisdiction of the court. In a prescient passage, Geoffrey Robertson has observed that:

> ... nobody occupying a position of *current* political or military power in any state (even one that has ratified the Treaty) is likely to be put on trial unless they invade another state and commit war crimes on its territory ... The class of criminal most likely to be arraigned by their state's consent at The Hague comprises persons who commit barbaric crimes in a cause which has utterly failed, in a country which decides to surrender them because it lacks the facilities to try them itself. In all other respects, the ICC will become a kind of 'permanent *ad hoc*' tribunal, dependent on references from the Security Council to investigate crimes against humanity in countries ... where none of the combatants have superpower support.

To a very large extent, the USA achieved its goal at the Rome Conference in that the ICC is very unlikely ever to prosecute a US citizen, even if the USA ratifies the treaty. The ICC prosecutor could in theory launch an investigation into crimes allegedly committed by US peacekeepers, but a case could only ever be heard in The Hague if the USA itself showed no interest in pursuing the case in a court martial or through the US domestic courts.[15] Moreover, the possibilities of the ICC prosecutor launching an investigation of crimes allegedly committed by an ally of the USA are exceedingly remote, given that it would require a referral from the state itself or from the Security Council, thereby requiring US support. For these reasons, President Clinton did eventually sign the Rome Statute, although no serious effort was made to ratify it. This meant that the statute was not legally binding, although under the terms of the 1969 Vienna Convention on the Law of Treaties, the USA was 'obliged to refrain from acts which would defeat the object and purpose' of the ICC. In effect this allowed the USA to adopt a wait-and-see attitude to the court. Some time in the future, when it is clear that it would never act against US interests, then a case might be made for ratification in Congress. The Bush administration has found even this unacceptable, however.

The response to the murder of some three thousand people in the al-Qaeda attack on the World Trade Center and Pentagon has been to declare war on terrorism. One aspect of this policy was to produce a list of terrorist organizations, which included the LRA.[16] Another has been to effectively set aside conventions and agreements that US governments have in the past sponsored and ratified. These include parts of the UN Charter, some of the Geneva Conventions and Protocols, and the Convention against Torture.[17] It has also exacerbated distrust of the ICC. On 25 September 2001 the Bush administration supported the American Servicemembers' Protection Act, which was intended to stop military aid to states choosing to ratify the Rome Treaty, and to use military force against any country that arrests US 'servicemembers' on ICC warrants. Initially, appalled European allies persuaded the White House to withdraw its support for the bill, but in May 2002 the administration announced that it would 'unsign' the Rome Statute, and Congress passed the American Servicemembers' Protection Act three months later. Aid to countries that have ratified the Rome Statute has continued, but a condition is that they enter into bilateral arrangements with the USA not to accept ICC warrants for US citizens. It can be argued that such arrangements are unlawful, but many countries have been compelled to comply, including Uganda. The USA has also, until very recently, refused to allow mention of the ICC in Security Council resolutions.

The US attitude to the ICC, like the US approach to discussions at the Rome Conference, has irritated other states. Although behind the scenes there has been some quiet cooperation with the court,[18] the public position of the administration has been openly hypocritical. No attempt has been made to disguise the premise that international laws are important to regulate the actions of the rest of the world, but that that they do not apply to the USA. The strategy backfired in that it appears to have encouraged many states to quickly ratify the Rome Treaty to demonstrate their independence. As a result the ICC was theoretically up and running from mid-2002, meaning that it potentially had jurisdiction over crimes committed after that date, although the construction of its building was still going on and most staff were not yet in place. This is an extraordinary development, but it would be a mistake to read too much into it. There has not yet been a radical change in international relations.

The criminal tribunals set up in the 1990s highlighted actual and potential problems in implementing international criminal prosecutions which have by no means been resolved. For obvious reasons, many government officials and diplomats still prefer political arrangements to the allocation of accountability. Even those with little to hide find it expedient to ignore the failings

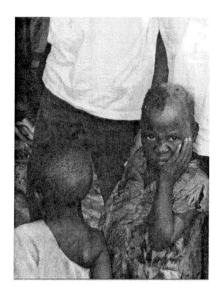

2 Does justice dissipate the call for revenge? A survivor from an LRA attack in Lira district (Tim Allen)

of others. There are also good reasons why impunity has so often been offered in the past, and not all those reasons went away with the end of the cold war. Most peace negotiations still involve some form of amnesty, even if it is linked to an 'outing' of the truth in a peace and reconciliation commission, such as occurred in South Africa. Moreover, ending impunity for the most egregious of crimes is not the same as establishing justice in a broad sense. It may not even be viewed as an ideal response to atrocities by surviving victims, or as a necessary aspect of making peace.

At the time of the setting up of the Hague Tribunal there was talk in the Security Council of 'healing of the psychological wounds',[19] and the resolution setting up the ICTR explicitly stated that it should help bring peace and reconciliation. The first president of the ICTY explained that: "Trials establish individual responsibility over collective assignation of guilt; ... justice dissipates the call for revenge, because when the Court metes out to the perpetrator his just deserts, then the victim's calls for retribution are met; ... victims are prepared to be reconciled with their erstwhile tormentors, because they know that the latter have now paid for their crimes.'[20]

But is this really so? Even if we leave aside the issue that indicting those alleged to be most accountable for terrible acts may preclude negotiations with the very individuals who could limit levels of violence, are prosecutions themselves therapeutic? Is it helpful to have a scapegoat, focusing anger and bitterness, and ameliorating divisions through ritualized public humiliation? Or does an international criminal trial have the opposite effect, making it clear why people should hate each other?

Would it not be better, as the Rwandan government has argued, if more locally relevant mechanisms of justice were deployed, so that those affected by crimes can themselves decide when it is appropriate to punish and when it is appropriate to forgive? Many analysts and activists responding to the ICC's intervention in Uganda would agree. One highly critical article refers to the dangers of 'international law fundamentalism' and proposes that:

> The decision, on the one hand, to seek justice through punishment or, on the other, to forgo punishment in favour of justice through reconciliation, is a decision that must be made by the concrete community that is the victim of the crimes and that will have to live with the consequences of the decision. 'Humanity' is too thin a community upon which to base a universal right to punish ... If local injustice is the price to be paid for the kind of international justice that results from ICC prosecution, then we must abandon the Court and imagine new modes of building a truly global rule of law.[21]

As we shall see, it is an example of the kind of view that the ICC has been unable to ignore. How it has responded is shaping what it will become.

2 | The coming of the Lord's Resistance Army

The LRA is commonly characterized in the Ugandan and international media as a barbaric and insane cult, with no discernible political agenda. Many expatriates employed in the region affected by the war share a similar view. They simply cannot understand how such a bizarre movement can have any credibility. They also rarely have any sense of how the current situation has come about. I was amazed when I returned to northern Uganda in November 2004 for the first time in many years to find that some foreign aid workers and journalists had never even heard of Alice Lakwena. So here too some background information is required.

A point often overlooked in discussion of this region of Africa is that war and mass forced displacements are even older than they at first appear to be. The lands of what has become the Uganda–Sudan border zone were devastated from the 1850s by armed traders and adventurers who reached this part of the Upper Nile from Khartoum. Their incursions were financed by the insatiable demand in industrializing countries for ivory – in order to make piano keys. The raiders were also interested in slaves, partly to carry the ivory north, and partly for the sexual gratification of themselves and their private armies. By the 1870s, the devastation was on a huge scale in local terms. The situation was then complicated further by the arrival of hundreds of 'Nubi' soldiers who were sent to the region to secure it for the Khedive of Egypt. Where possible, people sought the protection of war leaders who were able to act as local agents for the invaders, and many of the families that nowadays claim to be descended from pre-colonial traditional chiefs are in fact the descendants of such mercenaries. It is also worth noting that the pattern of abductions associated in recent times with the LRA has followed, even perhaps deliberately replicated, the depredations of the nineteenth-century raiders and their local allies.

Towards the end of the century the region was also affected by newly introduced bovine and human diseases, leading to further migrations and changes in livelihood patterns. After the Uganda Protectorate was set up in 1900, local wars continued until some degree of stability could be (violently) imposed in the years before and during the First World War. It was only at this time that most of the so-called 'tribes' were forged out of local clan groups, some of which recognized the former allies of the ivory traders as chiefs. In both the Anglo-Egyptian Condominium of the Sudan and the Protectorate of Uganda, the British administrations engaged such chiefs as agents. Where they did not exist, they were created. The British also used sleeping-sickness control programmes to move populations and concentrate them for administrative convenience. It was in this way that the Acholi and other 'tribes' that will concern us here were effectively constructed as separate population groups. The name Acholi may have been derived by British officials from the word for 'black' in the Lwo language (a language also spoken by other Ugandan groups that came to be classified as belonging to different 'tribes', such the Langi and Alur).[1]

The formation and classification of 'tribes' to some extent pre-dated the process of finally deciding where the border between Sudan and Uganda should be located. But this did not stop the boundary being constructed in such a way as to divide closely related populations. Some 'Acholi' groups were in fact deliberately included in Sudan, because the British officer from the Sudan administration who helped demarcate the boundary line thought their chiefs were quite 'progressive' and he wanted

26

to have some in 'his' territory, whereas the Ugandan official just wanted to go on leave, so he did not care one way or the other.

Under British rule, there were fifty years of relative peace on both sides of the border, but systems of indirect rule using gazetted local languages tended to institutionalize divisions, and give them an ethnic/tribal character. In Sudan this was compounded by the Southern Policy, introduced in the 1920s, which meant that the southern Sudan had a separate administration from that of the largely Muslim north. When independence was rushed through, war broke out in southern Sudan in 1955 (just before formal independence in 1956). It dragged on until the Addis Ababa Agreement of 1972 brought a decade of uneasy peace in most of the country. War in the south broke out again in 1983, however, and wars have also been waged in other regions, most notably in Darfur – as we all know from the recent media coverage of what has been called 'the first genocide of the 21st century'.[2] In the south, the Sudan People's Liberation Army (SPLA) and the government have recently been pressurized into peace negotiations and an agreement. This may well lead to the country dividing into two – although that is not what the SPLA says it wants.

No one would doubt that Sudan is a state in crisis.[3] Uganda, by contrast, has come to be regarded as a success story. This was not always the case, but since Yoweri Museveni seized power in 1986 Uganda has enjoyed economic growth and some degree of overall poverty decline. Controversial issues have generally been brushed under the carpet. The apparent invigoration of the Ugandan state is viewed as so important as to render any local inadequacies relatively unimportant. Even normally critical analysts of African governments such as Bayart, Ellis and Hibou can talk about Uganda as a place 'where the logic of violence has been replaced by political processes of negotiation and rebuilding'.[4] This hides a great deal.

Political upheavals, spirituality and guerrilla war

Uganda is a much smaller country than Sudan, but it has a population of roughly equivalent size that is as linguistically and ethnically diverse as its northern neighbour. In particular, there is a politicized divide between the groups of the north-west, the north, the south-west and the south, as well as between the old kingdoms, notably that of Buganda, and the rest of the country. These kinds of division were exacerbated by the indirect system of administration of the British Protectorate, and became linked to divisions between Protestants, Catholics and Muslims and to the multi-party political system introduced at the eve of independence.

Milton Obote, a Lwo-speaking Langi from the north, became the first Ugandan head of state, much to the chagrin of many in the south. He drew heavily on support from the armed forces, which had become dominated by northerners (partly because there were relatively few other employment opportunities in that part of the country and partly because the British had been eager to exclude the politically and economically powerful southerners). After a violent confrontation with the kingdom of Buganda in 1966, Obote became increasingly dictatorial, and increasingly dependent on his alliance with the army. It proved his undoing. In 1971, Idi Amin ousted him in a military coup.

The horrors of Amin's regime are well known. What is important to note in this context is that his own power base was in the north-west, and he quickly set about courting popular support in the south (at least initially) and in preventing any potential counter-coup from soldiers close to Obote. In particular, this meant removing Lwo-speakers from the armed forces. Soldiers from Lwo-speaking 'tribes', mostly Langi and Acholi, were told to report to barracks, where they were massacred. Thousands of Acholi and Langi fled the country, many becoming involved in campaigning against the Amin regime. Some formed the Uganda

National Liberation Army (UNLA) and, after Amin's invasion of Tanzania, they were provided with the opportunity for a serious military response. In 1979 the Tanzanian army, together with the UNLA and other affiliated forces, such as FRONASA led by Yoweri Museveni, invaded Uganda and overthrew Amin.

With Amin out of the way, and the remnants of his army defeated or across the border in Sudan or Zaire, elections were organized. These took place in 1980, but are widely asserted to have been rigged. Milton Obote's Uganda People's Congress (UPC) was declared the winner, and what is referred to as the Obote II regime began. Many anti-Amin activists, particularly from the south-west and south, refused to accept the results. In 1981, Museveni famously went to the bush with a small group of followers and founded the National Resistance Army (NRA). Obote's government was faced with guerrilla warfare inside the country, notably in Amin's home area in the north-west, and in the region to the north of the capital Kampala, known as the Luwero Triangle. He became completely dependent on the UNLA to keep him in power. The UNLA was nominally the national army, but again northerners made up a large part of it, predominantly (although by no means exclusively) from the Langi and Acholi 'tribes'.[5]

In the north-west, the activities of the UNLA forced a large part of the population to flee into Sudan as refugees. In Luwero such an option was not available to most rural people. Here the NRA was able to secure considerable local support, and the UNLA response was to treat most civilians as collaborators. They were herded into camps, and were frequently abused and killed. How many died is still a matter of debate, but it was certainly thousands. The killing went on in Luwero until Museveni seized power in January 1986, but Obote's regime did not last that long. In 1985, simmering tensions among Acholi in the army had burst into the open. The Acholi soldiers had various grievances, including the belief that they were the ones bearing the brunt of the fighting. Acholi soldiers seized power, and Tito Okello became president. He immediately started negotiations with Museveni and a peace agreement was signed in Nairobi. But the NRA proceeded to ignore it, and marched on Kampala – a source of deep-seated grievance among some Acholi, who claim that it shows President Museveni cannot be trusted.

After their defeat in the south, the Acholi soldiers retreated to their home area in the north. Some hid their weapons and tried to blend into the local population, but they found this difficult. It was well known that they had killed people in Luwero and elders were reluctant to perform the necessary healing rituals to allow them to be reintegrated into rural life. They also correctly foresaw that the victorious NRA and its allies would be eager to avenge UNLA oppressions. Many of the Acholi soldiers chose to move into Sudan to regroup. They were able to do this partly because there was an Acholi population in Sudan and their arrival was not altogether unwelcome. Many Sudanese Acholi were opposed to the Sudan People's Liberation Army (SPLA), perceiving it to be dominated by Dinka and other groups living to the north of their home area, so they joined or supported the Equatoria Defence Force (EDF), a militia resourced by the Sudan government. Acholi veterans from Uganda were a useful source of reinforcement.

Meanwhile, the National Resistance Movement's forces (the NRA and other integrated former-rebel groups) asserted control over the Acholi areas of Sudan, but just as in Luwero, experiences of persecution by the new government's soldiers helped create a fertile base for guerrilla activity. Many of the former UNLA soldiers formed anti-government groups, the most important of which was the Uganda People's Democratic Army (UPDA). This was all fairly predictable. Certainly Museveni could not have expected the Acholi population to welcome him with enthusiasm.

But then something really strange and unanticipated happened – spirit mediums emerged as military commanders.

An aspect of life for all the groups that have been studied by anthropologists in the Upper Nile (and indeed in much of Africa and elsewhere) is that understanding of affliction, including illness symptoms, is often interpreted in terms of interpersonal causes or relations with the spirit world.[6] This does not mean that understanding of empirical causality is absent, but that explanations for misfortunes tend to be pluralistic. A woman might say that she knows her child died of malaria, but she may still want to know why her child died and not her neighbour's. She may decide it was due to witchcraft or perhaps the involvement of the spirit world in the lives of the living. Therapy also reflects these ideas and a range of healers and specialists may be consulted as an alternative, or in addition to a bio-medically trained practitioner. During the mid-1980s, such ideas began to feed into Acholi armed resistance.

Under British rule enormous changes had occurred in Acholi society. Christianity and bio-medicine was introduced, chieftainship was promoted, labour migration and cash cropping became norms. In response there was a proliferation of different kinds of therapists who could explain and mediate these things. All patrilineages had their own shrines, where elders would invoke the spirits (*tibu* or *jogi*) of ancestors to interpret problems, but many changes seemed to be of a different order to anything that ancestors might understand. People turned to schoolteachers or Christian preachers for different sorts of advice, and also to individuals who seemed to have knowledge of strange and amoral forces (often associated with the 'outside', the 'forest' or the 'bush'). Among other things, responses were required to deal with wild spirits, which sometimes seized people and made them speak in strange voices or would cause particular afflictions (such as polio).[7]

Many of the specialists who emerged to deal with these phenomena were women or men who were in some way considered to be like women (perhaps because they were not married or were not living at their father's home). Female healers were appropriate partly because women are generally viewed as from the outside (a woman ideally leaves her father's home at marriage and travels to her husband's, then she will gradually change her lineage status to that of her spouse through the production of children and transfer of bridewealth). These new healers were called *ajwaki* (singular: *ajwaka*), the Lwo term for diviner, spirit medium or 'witch doctor'. Many of them were permanently possessed, but had learned to control their spirits and could call them at will to interpret various kinds of events. Some of them also asserted a strong Christian aspect to their healing, partly because their own experiences of the spirit world seemed to coincide with their interpretations of Christianity, but also to show that they were 'good' and that their spirits were pure (*tipu maleng*). These Christian diviners might call themselves *nebi*, the term used in the Acholi bible for prophets, to emphasize these qualities, and sometimes called their spirits *malaika* (angels). The Christian association was reinforced from the later protectorate period by the spread of Pentecostalism to the area, linked to the spread of the Balokole Protestant revivalist movement from other parts of East Africa (a prominent follower was Janani Luwum, an Acholi pastor who become an Anglican bishop and was murdered by Amin), and also by the attacks on 'witches' that occurred after independence in the mid-1960s.[8] In the 1970s, Islam and African/traditional healing were actively promoted by Amin's government, and this too had an influence, not least because the power of the established Christian clergy was weakened. There was further proliferation of forms of possession, and it became difficult to distinguish clearly between 'pagan' *ajwaki* and those that asserted the Christian or Muslim faiths, and might call themselves *nebi* or one of a number of other terms, such as *lapfwony* or *mwalimu* (teacher in Lwo and Swahili). At the same time, however, concerns about witchcraft and sorcery were intense, as the population tried to come to terms with the farther radical transitions and afflictions of the post-colonial era. So it became very important for possessed people to distinguish between bad/evil/Satanic/demonic/polluting spirits (*jogi marac*, *tipu marac, Satani, cen*, etc.), which needed to be exorcized, and good/clean/holy spirits (*tipu maleng, jogi maber, malaika*, etc.), which might have important messages and might intermittently possess their medium on an indefinite basis.

By the early 1980s, Christian (and sometimes Muslim) diviners or healers were common, as indeed were the possessions and other problems they were thought to be able to interpret and mediate. From mid-decade some of these healers were drawn into the political processes that were going on around them. In 1985, for example, just before the Okello coup, Acholi soldiers in the UNLA consulted and were blessed by a powerful *nebi* working near the Catholic mission hospital at Kalongo in Kitgum district called Angela Lamwaka. She condemned them, however, when they returned from the south with looted items, and predicted that they would lose power. Meanwhile, in Gulu town another *nebi* called Alice Auma had established a remarkable healing cult with a large following. It seems that she too had been approached by one of Okello's commanders in 1985. Interviewed in 1999, she claims that it was in fact her powers which enabled the coup to succeed, and that it was overthrown because her instructions had not been followed.[9]

Alice had become possessed by various spirits. These included Wrong Element (apparently from the USA) and a Muslim called Kassim. But the most potent was known as Lakwena, the Lwo term for messenger or apostle.[10] Her cult involved the use of water from the Murchinson Falls on the Nile, located in a national park near Paraa, many miles away from Gulu town. This had in fact been the site of an old cult, associated with a powerful spirit (*jok* or *jogi* in the plural) and a group of spirit mediums (*ajwaki*).[11] So Alice was linking her healing to a place with well-known, magical properties. Some sense of her local prestige can be gleaned from the fact that in 1985 two cars were at one point sent from the national park to collect various items and afflicted people from Gulu town and drive them to the falls. There they were taken into the waters and healed by Alice, assisted by her father, Sevarino Lukoya (who himself had at some point become possessed by God the Father – and still was when I met him in November 2004 in Gulu).[12]

In the upheavals that followed the victory for Museveni's forces in 1986, many other *ajwaki* and *nebi* emerged. Alice's cult, however, rapidly grew in significance. She performed healing rituals for UNLA soldiers after their retreat from the south, and through her, her spirits offered an interpretation of the UNLA defeat by the NRA that seemed compelling to many. She was able to cast out *cen*, the dangerous and polluting spirits of those who had been killed by the soldiers, and she loaded them with *malaika* (angels). She also explained that war is a form of healing through which people can be purified. The healing is on both sides, as those who die are like the rotten flesh cut out by a surgeon. The pure, on the other hand, cannot be killed.

According to Alice herself, her direct involvement in war started on 20 August 1986. She claims that the NRA soldiers kidnapped many young people of her age in the neighbourhood and imprisoned them at the barracks in Gulu town.[13] Their relatives begged her for help, and the Lakwena told her to recruit 150 soldiers. With the support of 150 former UNLA soldiers and forty guns, she says that she liberated the prisoners and that no one was killed or wounded in the attack. This was the start of a violent campaign against President Museveni's government, witches, other *nebi* and *ajwaki* and 'bad people', such as impure soldiers or individuals who did not obey certain rules or adhere to a complex range of rituals. Her movement came to be known as the the Holy Spirit Movement or the Holy Spirit Mobile Forces (HSMF), but to what extent this was originally her own term is unclear. In the Acholi bible, the term used for the third person of the Trinity is *Tipu Maleng*, but in other contexts this term can mean 'clean spirit' or 'clean spirits'. It could be that it was journalists reporting on the movement who introduced the explicit association with Christianity. Alice herself does not seem to have asserted that the Lakwena or any of her other spirits were the Holy Ghost. She nevertheless embraced the idea, perhaps because she and her commanders were eager listeners to the BBC World Service, which during periods of 1986 and 1987 was reporting daily on the HSMF's activities. In any case, ambiguities in manifestations of the Holy Ghost or Spirit in Acholiland had been common for some time owing to the activities of Balokole and other Pentecostals.

Alice's movement proved to be extraordinarily effective. At the end of 1986 she claims to have had 18,000 'soldiers'. She prayed with her followers at special sites called 'yards', and anointed them in oil, promising that if they were pure, bullets would not penetrate them. Among many other things, 'purity' included abstaining from sexual intercourse and alcohol. Soldiers in the NRA were confronted by scores of partly naked, glistening men and women marching towards them, some holding Bibles, others throwing magical objects, and a few wielding guns. In several encounters they seem to have been terrified or just did not know what to do. Initially, most ran away. Such early successes brought more and more recruits, with many former UNLA and UPDA soldiers joining her. In October 1987, she left Acholiland with around ten thousand followers, and led them south in a marauding crusade, overwhelming opposition on the way. They

35

were finally defeated in the swamps to the east of Jinja, some 80 miles from Kampala. Alice escaped on a bicycle, and has been living in a refugee camp in Kenya ever since. She claims that she abandoned her followers when they revealed impure tendencies during the march south. A large number died in the final assault, but some of those who survived managed to return to the north.

Back in the Acholi homeland, the UPDA continued its campaign from bases across the border in Sudan until it was drawn into negotiations. Most surrendered to the Ugandan government in 1988, but not all were prepared to accept the terms on offer. They joined a number of other groups, all of which were associated with men who were inspired by Alice Auma Lakwena's example.[14] The two most significant of these groups were movements connected with Sevarino Lukoya and Joseph Kony.

The first of these is Alice's father, a Balokole and former catechist of the Church of Uganda. He had had visions for some time and, as mentioned above, had participated in his daughter's cult of healing. Alice, however, is said to have converted to Catholicism shortly before or after the Lakwena possessed her, and she is reported to have rejected Sevarino's offer of assistance when she was leading the HSMF.[15] Only after her defeat did he begin his own military activities. Like Alice, he established ritual places called 'yards', where he would become possessed by Christian and Muslim spirits (he currently uses the Koran as well as the Bible in his services at his church/yard in Gulu). He claimed that some of his spirits came to him from Alice, including the Lakwena and Wrong Element (an unpredictable spirit which sometimes fought on the opposing side), and thus attracted some of her former followers. He established scores of yards in the Kitgum area and at one point had a following of about two thousand. Like Alice, he performed healing rituals and campaigned violently against other healers, killing several *ajwaki*

36

who he thought were pagan and impure. Unlike Alice, however, he encouraged his followers to become possessed too, so long as it was by what he regarded to be *tipu maleng* (clean/pure spirits). Possession was seen as a person being chosen to fight. He called his movement the Lord's Army. It was eventually defeated in 1989, and Sevarino spent some years in prison. He is currently living in Gulu, but has been building a house in Adjumani, the district to the west. It turns out that he had originally been a Madi but had migrated to Gulu and assumed an Acholi identity. Apparently the house in Adjumani will be for him and Alice, whom the Ugandan government have been trying to persuade to return home as part of the peace process (even paying her a sum of money to do so).[16]

Joseph Kony and the LRA

Joseph Kony has also asserted a kinship connection with Alice. It is often claimed that he is her 'cousin', or that they are from the same clan (*kaka*). Alice's father, however, was a Madi migrant, so the patrilineal connection cannot be as close as has sometimes been suggested. According to one source, Alice and Kony share a grandfather on their mothers' side.[17] They both seem to have spent their early life in the vicinity of Gulu town and Opit, and their most sacred shrines are not far from one another. Kony's family background is perhaps a bit vague because he comes from a family of male *ajwaki*. Although in the past male *ajwaki* were not uncommon, particularly where their cults were linked with patrilineal ancestor veneration, by the 1980s it had become unusual, and potentially very dangerous. As noted above, when it happens now, the men are often thought to be like women in some way, usually because they, or their father, came to live in a place as outsiders (i.e. they do not live on their patrilineal lands). So it is quite possible that Kony's father, like Alice's, was a migrant (or the son of a migrant).

The Lord's Resistance Army

Born in the early 1960s, Kony is two or three years younger than Alice Auma Lakwena. He dropped out of school after six years of primary education, and trained as an *ajwaka*, following the example of his older brother (and possibly also his father). When his older brother died, he inherited his powers (one informant, herself an *ajwaka*, told us that he actually killed his brother). At the time that the HSMF was active, Kony was possessed by a variety of spirits. In some accounts he claimed to have also been seized by the Lakwena as well as the spirit of Juma Oris, a former minister in Idi Amin's regime (whom Kony subsequently met in Sudan). Alice was mainly operating near Kitgum so Kony began recruiting soldiers and other followers near Gulu. He is said to have tried to form an alliance with Alice, but she rejected him, or rather she said that the Lakwena refused to accept him. Kony was apparently humiliated and his followers attacked and killed some of hers.[18] Kony also sought alliances with some of the other spirit cult movements operating to the west, but was again rebuffed. For example, his group ended up fighting with a movement led by a man called Philip Ojwok near Anaka (Ojwok's forces were intercepted by the NRA in 1988 and wiped out. Ojwok himself survived, however. Much to everyone's amazement he came out of the bush and surrendered in November 2004, having been living as a kind of hermit for the past sixteen years.)

Kony's early campaign was not a particularly significant affair, although with a small mobile group he maintained a degree of insecurity close to his home area. This changed, however, in 1988. In May, when President Museveni's government signed a peace agreement with the UPDA, many of those who were unwilling to surrender turned to Kony, including one of the UPDA's most ruthless and effective commanders, Odong Latek. From this point, Kony largely specialized in healing and divining, while Latek organized the forces. For a while, the group called itself the Uganda People's Democratic Liberation Army. Latek's influence on the movement was considerable, and Kony seems to have learned a great deal from the veteran commander about guerrilla tactics. His ally was killed in battle, but by 1990 Kony's force was the only significant armed unit still fighting in the Acholi homelands. Soon after Latek's death, Kony changed the name of the movement again, calling it the Lord's Resistance Army.

After his snub from Alice, Kony does not seem to have become possessed with any of her spirits again (although there are different views about this – one of my most knowledgeable informants is convinced that his power comes from having been seized involuntarily by Alice's most powerful spirit). Most informants say that Juma Oris became his chief spirit (something that must have caused some confusion when Kony was introduced to the living person). Other spirits are said to include a woman, Silindy Makay (sometimes called Silly Sindy), and Who Are You? (he apparently commands battle tactics by giving instructions through Kony). Like Sevarino Lukoya, Kony established 'yards' for cleansing and divining ceremonies. He has also followed Sevarino's example in drawing on ideas from Islam as well as Christianity (an aspect of his cult that became more prominent when he moved his bases north of the border in the second half of the 1990s),[19] and by being tolerant of other spirit mediums if they are vetted and found to be 'pure'. Those judged to be pagan *ajwaki* have been executed for Satanism and witchcraft. Kony, however, seems to have been keen to keep more personal direction of the activities and behaviour of his followers than Sevarino, so from the HSMF he took the idea of 'controllers'. These were a select group who had access to Kony when he was possessed and passed on instructions to followers, as well as checking compliance with various rules.

Continuing to work with a fairly small group, Kony's forces maintained a guerrilla campaign against the government and, increasingly, against anyone who collaborated with it.[20] The size of the LRA is a matter of speculation. One estimate from 1997 suggests as many as 3,000 to 4,000 combatants.[21] Others are much lower. The confusion arises partly because the size of the LRA has fluctuated and also because its main bases have been located in Sudan. The number of guerrillas actually operating in northern Uganda at any one time has rarely been more than a few hundred. Large numbers have not been necessary, because they have rarely engaged in pitched battles with government forces, but have used terror tactics to maximum effect. Like Alice, Kony claimed that Acholi society had to be purified by violence, but he has been much more prone to specifically target non-combatants.

His followers have also had a more ambivalent attitude to the Christian churches. Some Catholic priests have had a degree of access to him, but a priest has been killed and Kony at one point ordered attacks on missions. One of those priests who has been in touch with Kony is Father Carlos Rodriguez. He told me that:

> Talking and listening to Kony (on the radio) is a horrible experience. He talks normally for a while and says he is your friend, and then starts screaming in a high voice ... In May 2003 he said [i.e. told his followers] to kill all Catholic priests. Priests were attacked. Twelve missions were attacked in six weeks. I changed my place of residence every two days. When commanders told him of killings [of civilians] in Lira [district] he was laughing. He told them to kill more. He is mad ...

At the Catholic mission in Opit, the two Verona Fathers contrasted the behaviour of the HSMF and the LRA. One of them explained that:

> The Lakwena soldiers would come and ask us respectfully for flowers for their rituals. In July 1987 they were close by. Alice had her shrine five kilometres away. Then one day the NRA came

3 Father Carlos Rodriguez (on the left) and other Christian leaders have been among those who have tried to keep talks going with the LRA (anonymous)

through the bush. They said they were going to attack. Next day the Lakwena soldiers were singing and fighting. We went to see the bodies. There were heaps of them, some with stones in their hands and oil on their bodies. Some were naked. After a week the [NRA] soldiers came and closed the mission. We went to Gulu, but came back in 1994. In 1997, the LRA came. They shot at the door of our house [the father then took us to see the sixty bullet holes in their security door] ... In 1999 they came again. I hid myself in a store just three metres from the house and left the door open. They were looking for money. They stayed for one and half hours then went ... Another time they came at night. The church was full of people. They took fourteen girls and nine

41

boys. I went with them and met Odiambo [one of the LRA com-
manders], who contacted Kony on the radio. I spoke to Kony. He
talked about how Museveni was selling Uganda to Qaddafi. He
told us to go back home. I asked if the girls could go back too. I
brought them all back ... The parents were so happy ...

Other children have not been so lucky. A key strategy of the LRA
has been to abduct young people, including children, and to
educate them to be part of a new society, using forms of abuse
that are hard to believe. Many recruits become sexual slaves or are
deployed as combatants. Some are required to perform atrocities
against civilians in order to punish them for accepting President
Museveni's rule, demonstrate their loyalty and make it difficult
for them to return home because of the fear of reprisals. At peace
talks in 1994 (discussed below), Kony justified LRA actions to
those present as follows: 'If you picked up an arrow against us
and we ended up cutting off the hand you used, who is to blame?
You report us with your mouth, and we cut off your lips. Who
is to blame? It is you! The Bible says that if your hand, eye or
mouth is at fault, it should be cut off.'

In November 2004, I asked one young woman, who was herself
briefly abducted by the LRA from her secondary school dormitory,
why she thought young people have been captured and trained to
do these appalling things. Speaking in English, she replied: 'Why
the war has involved children? To me, I look at that child which
is young. Their minds can be eroded with a lot of things; it can
get caught up into the world that they see. They forget so much,
not like the adults ... The rebels ... target the children, because
they are brainwashed very fast ... and when they do something
they don't really reason: "What I am doing is bad" ... '

Although there have been claims that Kony is no longer possessed, the spiritual dimension of the movement has remained
important, continuing to instil both fear and respect for his

powers. Several of those who have spent time with the LRA told me that they were terrified Kony could read their minds and would kill them for thinking about running away. Others expressed continuing awe at his remarkable capacities. Kony's links with UPDA veterans, however, are reflected in some easing of restrictions on behaviour. The bans on consumption of certain kinds of food and alcohol seem to have generally remained in force, but sexual intercourse is used as a reward for loyal male followers. Certain abducted girls are selected as 'wives' – although it is important to note that sexual access to women has been regulated, and random rape has not been an LRA trait.

A secular element is also clear in the various LRA statements of demands. Generally they call for: (a) an all-party 'National Conference' followed by general elections; (b) creation of a Religious Affairs Ministry to 'see an end to the use of witchcraft and sorcery by promotion of the Ten Commandments'; (c) rehabilitation of the economy and rehabilitation of the country's infrastructure; (d) national unity (through inter-tribal marriages and language instruction); (e) education for all; (f) policies encouraging foreign investment; (g) the independence of the judiciary; (h) the formation of an ethnically balanced national army; (i) improved diplomatic relations with neighbouring states; and (j) relocation of Uganda's administrative capital to Kigumba in Masindi district.[22]

Manifestos and pamphlets listing these demands have appeared from time to time on the Internet and have been circulated in northern Uganda as printed leaflets. The LRA have also made efforts to make their points through broadcast media. In early 1999 an LRA radio station was set up, reportedly called 'Radio Free Uganda', which broadcast daily (presumably from Sudan) for a few weeks until the signal was blocked.[23] It accused President Museveni of overstaying in power and misusing funds, and demonstrated a familiarity with Ugandan and international politics, including such issues as the activities of the International Monetary Fund. It also broadcast denials of LRA involvement in the slave trade and allegations that hunger had made the rebels resort to cannibalism. Later, when Radio Mega was established in Gulu with a grant from the UK's Department for International Development towards the end of 2002, both Joseph Kony and his deputy, Vincent Otti, rang up during live broadcasts. The station immediately came under pressure from the government to stop it happening again. These initiatives by the LRA leadership indicate that it can make a more coherent political argument than most accounts allow, and suggest a desire to make a case to the Acholi population as a whole. This contradicts assertions that the rebels are all deranged and unaccountable for their actions. There are aspects to the LRA which draw on local understandings of the spirit world, and resonate with perceptions of 'the bush' (*olum*) as a place of unpredictable and amoral phenomena. But rational decisions have been made about policies, and terror has been a strategy of choice.

War and counter-insurgency strategies

From the time of the peace agreement with the UPDA in 1988, the Ugandan government, and President Museveni in particular, has persistently tried to downplay what has been happening. It seems to have been hard to accept that a spirit cult without a clearly articulated political agenda – or at least a very strange one – could sustain resistance against the well-organized and well-trained NRA. From the late 1980s, the war should have been over, and indeed the government frequently claimed that it was.[24] President Museveni's confidence that the northern problem was basically solved is reflected in the appointment in 1988 of a young Acholi woman as Minster of State for Pacification of Northern Uganda, resident in Gulu. It is hard to avoid the conclusion that the appointment of a woman with such a title was motivated by a

4 LRA soldiers posing with their guns: the youth squatting had just been abducted (anonymous)

5 LRA combatant and his 'wife' posing in the bush (anonymous)

6 LRA soldiers in the bush at night: note that those on the right are wearing Arab dress (anonymous)

7 Trying on a
new LRA uniform
in Juba, Sudan
(anonymous)

8 The LRA have
been included
in the Terrorist
Exclusion List of
the USA Patriot Act
of 2001: an LRA
soldier, probably
photographed in
Sudan, posing
with an Osama
bin Laden T-shirt
(anonymous)

9 LRA soldiers meeting with an informant. The rebels rely heavily on such intelligence-gathering in some areas (anonymous)

desire to show the president's power over Acholi masculinity, and was deliberately provocative. Predictably there were rumours that she was his lover. But things do not turn out as expected in this borderland. Kony succeeded in humiliating President Museveni and his armed forces, while Betty Bigombe proved more resolute and courageous than anyone could have imagined.

In 1991, irritated by the continuing insurgency, an intensive and brutal four-month military operation was mounted called Operation North, the main effect of which seems to have been to antagonize and alienate non-combatants. Betty Bigombe attempted to occupy a middle ground, trying to keep the door open for negotiation and restrict the NRA's depredations, but also introducing some vigorous anti-insurgency measures – such as arming community defence groups called 'arrow brigades'. The LRA's response, however, was ever more violent. Hundreds of people thought to be government collaborators were maimed or killed. LRA 'punishments' included the amputation of limbs and the cutting of lips, noses and ears. The NRA seemed reluctant to provide protection, and Bigombe's lightly armed 'arrow brigades' were especially vulnerable. The effect was to terrorize the population, and thousands of people sought refuge in the towns.

Nevertheless, in 1994 Bigombe's strategy of keeping a certain distance from all interest groups but being willing to talk to anyone seemed to pay off, and she managed to engage the LRA in peace talks. These seemed very promising. She went out into the bush without any protection for negotiations. Most of those who went with her on the first occasion were so terrified by the experience that they refused to go again. In the course of four more meetings with Kony, she arranged an uneasy ceasefire, and LRA soldiers were even able to visit and stay at some of the trading centres.[25] It looked as if there was a real prospect of a peace agreement. President Museveni's attitude to the talks, however, was not very enthusiastic, and at a political rally in February 1994 he humiliated Bigombe by issuing an ultimatum to the rebels. The LRA were given seven days to put down their weapons and turn themselves over to government forces. Within three days of the announcement, the killing resumed.

President Museveni has claimed that he had received military intelligence showing that the LRA were involved in peace negotiations only in order to build up their military capacity, and that they had secured assistance from the government of Sudan. Maybe this is true, but there were additional factors. Although expensive, the war in the north had certain political advantages for his government. The upheavals were contained in a part of the country in which he had no power base. In addition, the horrific violence and weird spirituality of the LRA allowed his government to present the north as a kind of barbaric periphery. He used this to present himself to people in the south as the guarantee that the oppressions of Amin, Obote and Okello would not return. President Museveni himself is from the south-west, and some people in Buganda were eager to replace him with someone else. But who else would protect them from the Acholi and other wild northerners? So it was not necessarily in President Museveni's interest to resolve the war by negotiation, and the much-publicized barbarism of the LRA had its political uses.[26] Moreover, by this time President Museveni had a personal grudge against Kony. The idea of offering a compromise to such a 'bandit' was hard to tolerate. Also, the war in the north kept the army occupied, and benefited many soldiers economically. Certain senior officers are well known to have become relatively wealthy from the situation.[27] It is, for example, an open secret that the army was involved in cattle rustling. In the past, Acholi families tended to keep their wealth in the form of cattle. By the mid-1990s, almost all of them had been stolen (the official explanation was that they were taken in raids by the Karamojong people of north-east Uganda). It was probably for a combination of all these reasons that President Museveni suddenly withdrew support for Bigombe's efforts.

Although there was little enthusiasm for the LRA among the Ugandan Acholi population, it had never depended on mass support, and from the period of the failed peace negotiations a generous line of assistance was indeed offered from Sudan. The Sudan government had decided to assist the LRA in retaliation for the Uganda government's barely disguised support for the Sudan People's Liberation Army (SPLA). In effect, the LRA became one of the many Sudan government militia through which it waged war in the south by proxy, and since the mid-1990s the LRA has been directly engaged in fighting the SPLA on behalf of President Omar Bashir's regime in Khartoum, as well as launching attacks into Uganda against the NRA and unsupportive civilians. For this, a much larger armed force has been necessary, and this is one of the reasons why the LRA expanded its policy of abduction. These abductions have striking parallels with the abductions of the slave and ivory raiders in the late nineteenth century, a point that is not lost on local people. With Sudanese support, the LRA was able to launch some of its most ferocious attacks. One of the worst single incidents occurred in May 1995, when the LRA burned scores of homes and killed almost three hundred people in Atiak, a trading centre just south of a large army barracks. On this occasion, as on so many others, the Ugandan government soldiers failed to respond until the rebels had already withdrawn.

A year after that massacre, the LRA announced a brief ceasefire during the Ugandan presidential elections. They even offered to stop fighting completely if President Museveni lost. In the event he won with a huge majority, although he received few votes in the north. Betty Bigombe had continued to maintain contact with the LRA after the collapse of the peace negotiations in 1994, and there were attempts made by a group of Acholi elders from Gulu to negotiate at the time of the elections, but these failed hopelessly (two elders were murdered by the LRA). Always a controversial figure, Bigombe was dropped from President Museveni's cabinet in June 1996 and promptly withdrew from a bruising by-election campaign with a young firebrand called Norbert Mao. She left Gulu and was replaced as minister by Owiny Dollo. Meanwhile Mao was elected to parliament and together with a group of other Acholi opposition MPs campaigned for the Ugandan parliament to formally investigate the situation in the north. After prolonged discussion, however, the inquiry ended up rubber-stamping the president's view that the military option should continue to be pursued. Further campaigns were launched, culminating with the first Iron Fist Offensive of 2002. Iron Fist has involved the Ugandan army, now called the Uganda People's Defence Force (UPDF), operating across the border in an open alliance with the SPLA.

International pressure had increased on President Bashir's government in Sudan during the late 1990s. The Clinton administration declared Sudan to be a terrorist state because of the government's alleged role in an assassination attempt on President Mubarak of Egypt, and for providing a base to Osama bin Laden – who was believed to be responsible for the bombings of US embassies in Kenya and Tanzania in 1998. By the end of the decade, President Bashir was trying to build bridges with his neighbours, and was doubtless alarmed by the US missile attack on what was asserted to be a chemical weapons factory in a suburb of Khartoum in August 1998. In 1999, his government decided to ask former US President Carter to become involved in the hope of normalizing external relations.

At this time there had been media coverage of abductions in northern Uganda by the LRA, notably of the 'Aboke girls' – a group of schoolgirls abducted by the LRA from their dormitory at St Mary's College in Lira district in October 1996 (they have been the subject of a television documentary and a book).[28] The Carter Center set about trying to persuade the Sudanese government to stop supporting the LRA, and managed to broker a deal between Presidents Bashir and Museveni whereby they agreed to stop supporting cross-border rebel groups (although in practice they continued to do so). International pressure on Sudan was nevertheless intensified following the attacks in the USA on September 11 2001. The LRA was added to the USA's list of terrorist organizations. There have also been more concerted efforts by the USA to broker a peace agreement with the SPLA (perhaps partly motivated by growing interest in Sudan's oil reserves). As a consequence the Sudan government has been forced to give permission for the Iron Fist incursions from Uganda since 2002, although it continues to have an interest in protecting and even supporting the LRA as part of the complex manoeuvrings around the Sudan peace process.

President Museveni himself has directed some of the Iron Fist campaign from a base in the north. With US logistical support, and using helicopter gunships, an estimated 10,000 Ugandan troops have been involved. LRA bases in Sudan have been destroyed and hundreds of people killed. Understandably, the Ugandan government has called those who have died 'rebels', but it is clear that many have been abducted people, including children. Kony and almost all his senior commanders, however, evaded capture. Some retreated deeper into Sudan while others

51

divided into small units and moved south of the border. As fast as abducted people died or were captured/freed, more were taken. If Operation Iron Fist of 2002 really was aimed at resolving the situation once and for all, it has to be judged a failure.

The LRA was allowed to outflank the UPDF/SPLA forces and had almost a free rein in northern Uganda, moving into new territories and perpetrating new massacres, notably in Lira district, but also in Soroti, Apac and Katakwi. In October 2002, LRA groups back in Sudan were still potent enough to help the Sudan government forces recapture the town of Torit from the SPLA. Given the apparent investment in Iron Fist, it is hard to avoid the suspicion that the Ugandan government had other agendas. Doubtless the LRA capacities were underestimated, but also many of the troops used had recently returned from Uganda's controversial intervention in the Congo. They were allegedly infected with diseases and ill disciplined. Some analysts have argued that President Museveni just wanted them out of the country.[29] The Sudan government agreed to a second Iron Fist offensive from March 2004. This has proved to be rather more effective, and is one reason for the increase in LRA fighters accepting amnesty (see Chapter 4). The LRA has continued to operate from bases in Sudan, however, almost certainly with a degree of continued assistance from the Sudan government, and is still capable of attacking camps in Uganda as well as isolated groups of Ugandan government forces.

3 | Displacement and abduction

The effects of the LRA campaign and the Ugandan government's response have been catastrophic for the local population. Much of Gulu, Pader and Kitgum districts have been abandoned. Neighbouring areas, such as eastern Adjumani district and parts of Lira district, have also been affected. The movement of people to towns and close to garrisons has become a permanent arrangement, and from late 1996 became an integral component of the Ugandan government's anti-insurgency policy. In some places, anyone who refused to move from their rural homes was forcibly displaced (a policy that seems to have been modelled on the internment centres that had been created by the UNLA in Luwero in the early 1980s). In early 1997 World Food Programme food relief was delivered to 110,000 people in 'protected' IDP (Internally Displaced Persons) camps. Two years later the number had risen to over 400,000, and by mid-2002 to 522,000.[1] The numbers then escalated dramatically as a consequence of the LRA incursions during the first Iron Fist offensive. Around 80 per cent of the population of the three Acholi districts (Gulu, Kitgum and Pader) now live in camps. The rest live in the main towns or have moved to other regions. The total number of people living in IDP camps peaked at about 1.5 million in 2004. Overcrowded, spatially constrained, lacking adequate water, and heavily dependent on relief food, the camp's conditions are almost universally grim and in some instances appalling.

Living in IDP camps

Until recently, the security of people living in the camps was very low. In 2005, it remains very unpredictable. Each camp was

10 Awere IDP camp on the border between Gulu and Pader districts. The picture shows the concentration of settlement in the camps. Fires are a constant threat (Elliott Green)

supposed to have an army detachment, but the soldiers have notoriously failed to respond or have run away whenever there has been an attack. A small amount of cultivation is possible in the immediate vicinity, but even this is risky. Anyone who wanders too far is in danger of abduction or being accused of collaboration with the rebels (or in some places of losing a leg to a landmine). Usually the LRA attack at night, sometimes operating right in the heart of the camp. To avoid abduction, thousands of young people commute to the bigger towns or to the centre of the camps in the evening, sleeping in schools and dispensaries, on the verandas of shops or at the Catholic missions. For young women, in particular, this has sometimes exposed them to abuse. Transactions occur in certain places whereby accommodation is offered in return for sex.[2] Various aid agencies have also established night commuter centres. Watching the daily movement to these places can be astonishing. Vast numbers of children carry their blankets along the roads in the evening, in some cases for long distances, returning to their IDP camp or the urban suburbs in the early morning, ideally in time for school. On 1 April 2004, a survey of eleven night commuter sites in Gulu town found almost 20,000 children.[3] The numbers vary depending on how recent the last attack has been. Figures from one site, Lacor hospital, show a rise from 3,000 in December 2003 to 6,000 in March 2004.

Although there have been some improvements in the protection afforded to the camps since the major incidents of early to mid-2004, they remain vulnerable, particularly at night. In March 2005, I was staying at Atiak IDP camp when a group of LRA launched an attack in the early evening, quite close to the centre. The local UPDF responded, and a short exchange of fire ensued, with casualties on both sides. The events that followed were very revealing. The UPDF soldiers moved around the camp shouting at people in Swahili. Then they made everyone put out fires and lights, and anyone found moving around near the main street was beaten. The soldiers were clearly in a panic and their behaviour unpredictable and potentially dangerous. In the morning, the body of an LRA combatant who had been killed was still lying in the road. No one had been allowed to cover him with leaves, as is the custom, and his body was being eaten by the local pigs. Many Acholi believe in *cen* (a polluting spiritual force), which afflicts those exposed to violent death with nightmares and illnesses. So in this way, it seemed, the camp population were being terrorized and punished for what had happened.

In general, the worst public health situation tends to be in the newer camps, which can have extremely poor sanitation. Outbreaks of cholera are, however, not confined to these. Atiak is one of the oldest camps, but continues to have outbreaks.

11 Pagak camp
after it had been
set on fire in 2004
(anonymous)

A survey of new camps in Pader and Lira was carried out by MSF-Holland in 2004.[4] It found a 'severe acute malnutrition rate' of 4.4 per cent, and a 'global acute malnutrition rate' of 8.28 per cent among children aged 5–59 months.[5] These figures are comparable to those for other areas of northern Uganda. But the survey also collected mortality and morbidity data. The overall Crude Mortality Rate (CMR) was 2.79/10,000/day (above 1 is generally categorized as an emergency rate) and the under-five mortality rate was found to be an astonishing 5.4 (in one camp, Agweng, it was found to be 10.46). The main causes of reported morbidity were malaria/fever (47 per cent), respiratory diseases (28 per cent) and diarrhoeal diseases (21 per cent) – all closely

12 Pigs
scavenging around
overflowing pit
latrines at Agweng
IDP camp in Lira
district. It is hardly
surprising that the
mortality rate in
the camp is so high
(Elliott Green)

13 Waiting for the water pump to be turned on at Atiak IDP camp in Gulu district. Collecting a full container can take hours. The alternative is a filthy stream (Tim Allen)

associated with the living environment. 'Malaria' was the main reported cause of death, followed by 'diarrhoea'. When I first saw these data, I found the CMRs hard to believe, but on visiting the particular camps surveyed, I was shocked. People were living in some of the most appalling conditions I have seen in many years of working in war- and famine-affected regions. In July 2005 a further survey was carried out, this time under the auspices of the World Health Organization (WHO).[6] It was designed to be representative of all IDPs in Gulu, Kitgum and Pader districts. The CMR for all IDPs was found to be 1.54, and the under-five CMR was 3.18. Figures were worst in Pader district, which had a CMR of 1.86 and an under-five CMR of 4.24.

Displacement and abduction

Various studies have also drawn attention to other aspects of the atrocious quality of life in the IDP camps. For example, an MSF-Holland survey on mental health in Pader town found that 79 per cent of people had witnessed torture, 40 per cent had witnessed killing and 5 per cent had been forced to physically harm someone; 62 per cent of women interviewed think about committing suicide.[7] Other studies have drawn attention to similar issues, with several giving particular emphasis to sexual violence, including rape and other forms of abuse by government soldiers, and raising concerns about HIV/Aids.[8]

Alarming information about the spread of the epidemic appears in both aid agency and media reports, and is often confirmed by people living in the IDP camps themselves.[9] It is not uncommon to be told something like, 'We all have Aids. Can't you see that we are so thin and dying?' Some will even quote bits of data that they may have read or heard on the radio. Here is a comment from one young woman (speaking in English):

> I think the result of this war, what the community will experience will be ... HIV [because of] the rape. If you compare the Uganda statistic, it's only 6 per cent, but when we look at northern Uganda and other places it's already doubling the Uganda statistic, it's 12 per cent ... Even among the children, there are very many affected ... though it has not yet come out physically ... the result it is only going to be something [seen] with the time. The war that we will see will be the war with HIV; we will really have to fight that after [this one ends].

These kinds of view are understandable, but should be treated with caution. It is not clear that rape and sexual violence are worse in northern Uganda than in other parts of the country. Life in the IDP camps is tightly regulated, and there is little privacy. Moreover, incidents of sexual activity in themselves may not be linked closely to an increase in transmission of HIV. It depends, in part, on the sexual links between those who are HIV positive and those who are HIV negative.

Antenatal surveillance data from Lacor hospital near Gulu town give a prevalence of over 11 per cent. This is slightly higher than similar data from sentinel sites in other parts of the country, but is a very significant decline from the prevalence of 27 per cent recorded at Lacor in 1993.[10] Elsewhere in the war zone, antenatal rates have been recorded by one of the international NGOs, AVSI, at hospitals in Kitgum and Kalongo, Pader district. Prevalence rates vary from 4.6 to 9.9 per cent. It is interesting to note that the lowest rate was recorded at Kalongo, which provides services to more rural areas.[11] These rates are similar to those in other parts of northern and central Uganda. From these and other indicators it would appear that the concentration of people in the IDP camps has actually coincided with a decline in rates of infection, not a rise. It also needs to be reiterated that the LRA has not raped its victims indiscriminately. Combatants are expected to abstain from sex unless given permission.[12] Some of those girls abducted have been selected as 'wives', and a World Vision report has suggested that such use of sexual bondage as a weapon of choice by the LRA increases prevalence rates.[13] This is not, however, supported by the available evidence. In so far as data are available, it seems that returned abductees are no more likely to be HIV positive than the rest of the population.[14] The main risk factor appears to be proximity to urban centres.[15]

The whole system of population displacement into camps, which has both caused extraordinary suffering in itself and has failed to provide adequate protection, can be maintained only with donor assistance. Reluctantly various agencies became involved in providing food to the camps set up in the mid-1990s. Initially it was a relatively small operation, but it has grown. By 2003 this was probably the biggest IDP population in the world. It happened almost without being noticed. When Carol

Bellamy, then the executive director of UNICEF, visited in May 2004, she was appalled. She talked about the 'need to wake up to the enormity of the crisis' and it being a 'moral outrage'.[16] Yet the situation is as much a product of well-meant aid as the controversial negotiated-access relief programmes in the war zones of Sudan. These have contributed to what David Reiff calls 'a crisis of conscience among sensible humanitarian agencies'.[17] In Uganda, the achievement of President Museveni's government in transforming the country into a relatively viable state has meant that the contradictions in providing aid during an ongoing war have not been fully addressed. The very success in effectively absorbing development finance has, in this part of the country, drawn international organizations into long-term, institutionalized arrangements with anti-insurgency strategies. People in the IDP camps live in a place of extraordinary structural violence. The issue of ending impunity in the Rome Statute, with its inherent rejection of compromises made with the perpetrators of crimes, including 'forcible transfer of population', cuts to the core of the dilemma. Perhaps some of the local hostility to the ICC is to do with disquiet about established dispensations. There is no doubt that they need challenging.

Living with the LRA

Accurate data for the scale of abduction by the LRA is unavailable. This is partly because systematic registration of abducted people by local councils and community volunteers began only in 1997, and it has been haphazard since 2001. Even for the 1997–2001 period, the accuracy of the data has been questioned. It may be that incidence of abduction was underestimated, perhaps because families wanted to keep it secret. People who have been with the LRA are supposed to be questioned at a barracks on their return, where some report being treated harshly or being placed under pressure to join the army. Alternatively, the data

14 Aid agency vehicles, some of them armour plated, make forays out to the IDP camps. Relief operations keep the whole system going. But is this really the best strategy? (Elliott Green)

may have overestimated incidence, because they do not specify how long someone must be away to be recorded as abducted, and it is unclear whether people can be recorded more than once.

Another problem is that the term 'abduction' suggests innocence and a lack of agency. It conveys the idea that being with the LRA has no element of choice, and that those returning should be the recipients of sympathy. They are not 'collaborators' or 'sympathizers'. In many cases this is correct, but in other cases things are less clear. For example, at Atiak, a place close to the border with Sudan, the population has to cohabit with groups of LRA who frequently move around the camp. Sometimes people are told to give them food or carry things, and are then released. They are not always forced to become combatants or 'wives'. Many people have been abducted in this way a number of times.[18] Several informants told me that they have been abducted on four or five occasions, always for brief periods. Others have talked about locally active members of the LRA being childhood play-mates, and seem to have a kind of ongoing relationship with them. Use of the term abduction ignores these complications.

Moreover, formerly abducted people have been the focus of assistance projects, such as the provision of food and other items. There are therefore positive incentives to be registered. This is well illustrated by the results from a large-scale survey using a structured questionnaire carried out in April and May 2005.[19] Of the 2,585 randomly selected adults who were interviewed in Gulu, Kitgum, Lira and Soroti districts, 40 per cent claimed to have been abducted, and 31 per cent claim to have had a child abducted. In Gulu and Kitgum the figure for adult abduction was over 50 per cent and for children 38 per cent. It is hard to know how to interpret these findings. If abduction is taken to mean that people have spent time with the LRA and have been drawn into their activities, then it suggests that it is a mass movement with widespread grassroots involvement. That is clearly not the case. It is interesting, however, to note the higher number of adult abductions than those for children. This is also reflected in the most robust abduction data available.

A survey of all abductions, reported through local councils and community volunteers between 1997 and 2001, was carried out by UNICEF in 2001 (including short abductions of just one day). It found that a total of 28,903 people had been taken from Gulu, Kitgum, Pader, Apac and Lira districts between 1990 and 2001.[20] The most intense period of abduction during this decade occurred soon after the failed peace negotiations, with over 6,000 reported abductions in 1996 (including the famous Aboke girls). Fewer than 10,000 of the reported abductions (less than a third of the total) were abductions of children (i.e. people under eighteen). The largest number of abductions was of people aged eighteen to thirty-five (about 45 per cent). The overall majority of those abducted were male (about 70 per cent). By the end of 2001, about 16,000 abducted people had returned (i.e. they had escaped, had been freed by the LRA or they had surrendered or been captured by the Ugandan army). Just under 13,000 were still missing (i.e. still with the LRA or dead), of which 5,555 were thought to be children. The vast majority of those who had returned had done so within a year of their abduction (almost 80 per cent). After these data were collated, the security situation declined drastically, making it impossible for systematic monitoring to be sustained. Numerous further abductions occurred, estimated by local UNICEF staff at between 10,000 and 15,000. It is possible that patterns of abduction may have changed during the past four years, partly reflecting a high fertility rate and low life expectancy. A household survey in June 2005 found that less than 17 per cent of the population of Gulu, Pader and Kitgum districts was above the age of 35.[21] The WHO mortality survey of July 2005 found that all twenty-eight of the abductions since the beginning of the year that were reported by respondents in the sample had been of persons under thirty-five, and that 46.6 per cent were of children below the age of fifteen.[22] The best available current estimate of how many children abducted from Uganda are still with the LRA (i.e. excluding children that the LRA may have abducted in Sudan), based on security information and numbers reporting at reception centres, is a total number of around one thousand.[23] There is no reliable estimate for the number of abducted adults who are still missing.

While recognizing the weaknesses in these data, we must stress some important points. The scale of child abduction has been terrible, and so have the experiences of some of those who have been abducted. But this has not been the only form of recruitment to the LRA, and numbers of children involved in the perpetration of violence have often been overstated. There is no doubt that many combatants in the LRA have been recruited as teenagers, and that quite a large proportion of these have also been under the age of eighteen. But most of those who have actually been fighting seem to have been adults. I have not been able to find evidence that over 85 per cent of recruitment to the LRA is made up of abducted children – a figure that has appeared in many reports and articles and is even repeated in the ICC press release of January 2004 on the situation in Uganda.[24]

During a visit to northern Uganda, Jan Egeland, the UN Under-Secretary-General for Humanitarian Affairs, is reported to have said that, 'This is not a normal guerrilla war between rebels and a government. This is a war on, and with, and against children.'[25] A problem with this sort of interpretation is that it implies that in some way the LRA combatants are not accountable for their actions (because they are abducted and traumatized children). In fact, the LRA have been using approaches adopted in many other wars, especially since the early 1990s.[26] According to the UNICEF data up to 2001, the percentage of children among those abducted in northern Uganda was actually less than in the south-west, where another Ugandan rebel army called the Allied Democratic Front has operated since the mid-1990s.[27] It is also worth noting that the LRA has abducted relatively few women. The impression has sometimes been given that girls are more vulnerable than boys, partly because of the publicity and concern focused on those abducted from St Mary's College, Aboke, in 1996.

This is not to suggest that the suffering of abducted children has been anything other than terrible. The point is that the abduction of children has been a deliberate strategy – a weapon of choice. Like rape, it has been used systematically and selectively to terrorize the population. Indoctrinating impressionable young people and making them do terrible things, such as kill their own parents, inverts the moral order and shows the power of the LRA. Releasing some children and adults soon after their capture is part of this process. Their stories are meant to instil respect and fear, by demonstrating that returning home, like mutilation and death, is at the whim of a commander. The very unpredictability of what can happen after capture is part of what makes it so alarming. Moreover, there is no doubt that the LRA targets children during attacks. Scores of babies have had their skulls crushed with clubs and toddlers have been thrown into fires. Again, the purpose is to terrorize. It has been very effective – evidenced by the scale and persistence of night commuting.

In sum, experiences of abduction vary widely. Sometimes people are abducted in order to carry food that the LRA has looted from fields or from displacement centres after its distribution by the World Food Programme. These people may have to carry their burden for long distances, and they are likely to be beaten or worse. Once the food has been taken to a secure place, however, many are released. Other captives are taken for training as LRA combatants, or used as sexual slaves. Those chosen are mostly in their late teens or early twenties. The women appear to be selected for their attractiveness and intelligence. They are often given as 'wives' to much older men as a reward, mostly commanders or individuals who have proved themselves in action.[28] Joseph Kony himself has 'married' more than forty abducted girls. Those people who are not quickly released by the LRA are forced to undergo brutal initiations. These include anointing with oil, very severe beatings and usually participation in killings. Even those girls taken as sexual slaves or 'wives' are often made to help kill at least one person.

I have found that people who have been taken and kept by the LRA can be willing to recount their stories in extraordinary detail. Once they realize that someone is prepared to sit and listen, they go into an almost trance-like state and give their account as a monologue from beginning to end. Stopping and asking questions sometimes seems to disconcert them. They want to explain what happened to them in their own way. Several spoke to me without a break for, literally, hours. In the remainder of this chapter I shall convey an impression of this material with some extracts. These have been selected to make various points, and they are not the result of a systematic study based upon a sampling procedure. They give a vivid impression of what can happen to those forced to join the LRA. All the interviews took place in Lwo. Where necessary I have inserted questions to make the quotes comprehensible.

Some experiences of abduction

From an interview in Kitgum with a woman in her twenties:

... When I was abducted I was in our home in Purongo. I walked up to Sudan before returning to my village again. I tried to escape but unfortunately I was caught and brought back among other abductees. At first they wanted to kill me but I pleaded with them, telling them I was the only survivor of my late parents, so I was only caned. After that we went back to Sudan, I was about twelve years old at the time ... On reaching there I was given to a man as a wife. I tried to resist but I was threatened with death so I had no option other than to accept. None the less my stubbornness bought me two hundred strokes of the cane before I was handed over to my new husband. Later I was trained for a year and returned to Uganda as a fighter despite the fact I was pregnant by then. Unfortunately I got injured ... I also had a miscarriage as a result. Later I was given the rank of second lieutenant. This was for motivation and because I had taken a long time in the bush, and maybe as a reward for good work since I used to clean the wounds of the injured, and also help to train the newly abducted children on how to take care of themselves while in the bush. I had to stay for twelve years in the bush ...

Why did the LRA mutilate people?

People's lips were cut off because it was with the lips that they made alarms when being under attack and they [the LRA] also claim it was the same lips that people use for reporting them to the UPDF, who pursue and attack them. So this was done to discourage others from making an alarm when being pursued. And the rest of the other body parts were cut on the same argument that they aided the civilian to contact the UPDF ...

What did you think of Kony?

Kony has got some spirit in him that reveals to him what others cannot see. For instance, he can foretell what would happen next. You could imagine Kony is not educated at all but bright and educated people follow him not in fear but rather in obedience to his orders ... Kony is a normal man when not under the influence of the spirit but when possessed his eyes turn red and his voice also changes ...

The next extract comes from an interview in Gulu town with a twenty-year-old woman. She was living in hiding after her escape from the LRA. The brothers of her mother had attacked her at her father's home, because she had killed their sister:

Why did you kill your mother?

... I was abducted from Pabbo in April 1990 over the weekend as I was going to the garden to help my mother. It was around 7.30 in the morning when I was abducted together with my mother. We only moved a short distance away and I was then asked to kill my mother. I first refused but I was told my mother will be asked to kill me. They kept insisting. They tried to force my mother to kill me, but she would not. They said they would kill both of us, but my mother told me that I must kill her to survive. I did it, but I loved my mother. I wanted both of us to die. After that I moved with them ... Around August 1991 we entered into Sudan. I was trained as a soldier. We used to go and raid food and clothes from the Dinkas [i.e. SPLA] in Sudan ... In 1993 we came to Uganda, and stayed around Kitgum ... From 1993 to 2000 my work was to carry tins of bullets ... I escaped in September 2000 ... After all those years that I stayed in the bush I came back without a child. I stayed in the bush for nine years. My 'husband' used to beat me, saying that I was only refusing to have a child ...

What do you think of Kony and his special powers?

I met Kony face to face when they passed us out as newly recruited soldiers. He told us to be strong hearted and fight for the
freedom of Acholi people. It's our duty to free the Acholi whose
land will be taken away by Museveni. Later a stone was burnt
into ashes with oil *'moo yaa'* and smeared on to our bodies. Also
water was sprinkled on us. Then Kony said from that time we
are his soldiers ... They smeared us in this way for protection
and to make us strong. It was also to stop us escaping. We were
told that if we escaped, the holy spirit [*tipu maleng*] would bring
us back ... I believed it. When I was still there, this made me so
scared that whenever my heart told me to escape I would say to
myself that the spirit is looking at me. Then I just gave up ...

The next extract is from an interview with a former LRA soldier
who had been abducted at the age of ten and stayed in the bush
for eight years. The Ugandan army had recently captured him after
he was wounded in an engagement. The interview took place at
the World Vision reception centre in Gulu in November 2004.

*Did the commanders ever explain why they were attacking the
camps?*

Yes, the commanders said the Acholi people were stubborn
and did not want to support their movement since they encourage their children to escape when they are abducted. So they had
to kill them to make them learn.

*Why were the rebels cutting off people's legs, lips and other body
parts?*

That happened when I was still in Sudan but I learnt from
some friends that it was some spirits that ordered Kony to do
that; for instance, cutting the legs of those caught riding bicycles
and cutting the lips of those who tried to make alarms.

The following extract is from an interview with a boy of about seventeen, interviewed at Atiak displacement camp. He too was asked about killing and gave a very frank and gruesome answer.

After I was abducted I stayed with the rebels for six months. It feels good to be back with my mother, but I still have pain in my body from the beatings ... I was tied and beaten many times ... For most of the time I was not fighting, because I was small. They sent me up high trees. I had to stay there to watch for the soldiers ... I moved with the rebels from place to place ... but they never stopped beating me. Even if they see you eating without permission you are beaten ... They also forced me to kill many times ... So many times that I cannot remember how many ... If you refused to do the killing [with a club or panga] they would cut off the head and make you carry it. They said that the *cen* [polluting spirit] of the dead person would possess us and that it would mean that we could never go home ... None of us wanted to carry the head, so we all had to kill ... When the killing is done, each of us had to swallow some of the blood ... This was as a kind of cleansing ... The head was passed around and we all had to taste the blood ... Some of the people we killed were people who had tried to escape ... Not all the commanders make their soldiers do this ... It depends on the person ... We had someone with us who was an expert at killing ... He was a man called Odong who had lost one of his eyes ... He is an old man and still alive out there in the bush ... The commanders were the lucky ones ... they have [magical] protection and the guns cannot affect them ... Even if you stand next to them, the bullet will hit you but not them ... My sister was also abducted with me, but she was taken away and I have not seen her since then ...

The above informant went on to explain how he managed to escape, but the interview was interrupted when we heard gunfire. The local army detachment had ambushed a group of LRA who were approaching the displacement camp to steal food, killing

15 A picture drawn by one of the people staying at the Rachele reception centre for those formerly abducted by the LRA in Lira town. The artist claimed to have witnessed or been made to participate in each of the acts depicted (Tim Allen)

one of them. The mother of the boy was also present. She and one of his younger brothers had been wounded in an attack, leaving the woman crippled. In a neighbouring home we had just interviewed another mother, surrounded by the graves of her children. They had all been hacked to death in much the same way as described above (possibly by the boy we interviewed).

The details about the cutting off of heads relate to old customs among some Acholi groups linked to the allocation of social status to a person who had killed, and to rituals necessary to contain the effects of the polluting spirit (*cen*) of the deceased. In his ethnography of the Acholi, Girling describes how a warrior would cut off the head of someone he had killed and take it to his ancestral shrine to show what he had done, and then be blessed and treated. A complicated ritual was performed and a girl was symbolically given to him as a wife. After several days of ritual ablutions to ensure that *cen* had been purified, the man would be given a special praise name and cuts would be made on his right shoulder to indicate what he had done.[29]

Lastly, here is an extract from an interview with a young woman who was abducted from St Mary's College in Lira district in 1996, but was lucky enough to be quickly released. After her abduction by the LRA she managed to continue her education, and is now living in Gulu town (she spoke in English).

How has the war affected you?

Actually war has affected us in many ways. We can't move to the villages really to share the joy that we used to have with the village people. The moral path has really been degraded so much that you find children moving from their places [i.e. not staying with their parents]. They don't really get ... what people used to get in their communities, sitting together around the fireplace and trying to discuss and get the moral education from their parents.

Have you been surprised by the way people have behaved?

I have really been so surprised because when I look at women, always they say that women have forgiveness and a peaceful heart. But in this war I look at it as the contrary of this, the other side of the coin. Because ... the atrocities, the fighting and the heartless things being done are inflicted by women and children ... They are killing and ... being rude to people in captivity. One of the girls, Jane, told me when she was just abducted, the first welcome she had was by a woman, and she was given 250 strokes with the cane. She thought that this girl would really have sympathy for her being abducted; instead she was jealous that she had come to take away the husband that had been given to her. So I am really so surprised because to me I think of women as having a heart full of forgiveness ...

71

4 | Amnesty, peace talks and prosecution

By the end of 2004 it seemed that, after eighteen years of war, things might be about to change. Processes were occurring that offered alternatives to institutionalized population controls and counter-insurgency measures. First, after a great deal of activism from civil society groups, NGOs and concerned politicians, an amnesty had been offered to the rebels. Second, efforts to negotiate a ceasefire and restart talks had begun to produce results. Third, President Museveni had referred the situation in northern Uganda to the ICC and criminal investigations by the Office of the Prosecutor were under way. A problem, however, was that the latter appeared to undermine the other two. If there were going to be prosecutions, what was the point of the amnesty and on what basis could there be negotiations? This chapter discusses these developments. To begin with they have to be placed in political context.

The change in political context

One important factor had been the changing attitude of the USA. It had not in the past played a very significant role in northern Uganda, but the inclusion of the LRA in the Terrorist Exclusion List of the USA Patriot Act of 2001 suggested that more should be done, and this had included some assistance for Operation Iron Fist. President Museveni's government and the UPDF had invested a great deal in the offensive across the border in Sudan, but (at least initially) it failed. Far from ending the war by the end of 2002 as promised, the fighting spread into new areas and the scale of displacement in northern Uganda was massively increased. The military option seemed not to be working.

The Ugandan government explained the failure by arguing that the LRA had continued to receive support from Sudan, in spite of the agreement brokered by the Carter Center, as well as from Acholi in the diaspora (i.e. Acholis living in rich countries). President Museveni's international prestige was adversely affected, however, and by late 2003 explicit statements were being made by some of Uganda's main aid donors about the need for a change of strategy. The EU referred to 'reservations about the military option' and the UK's deputy high commissioner is reported to have said the 'war effort has failed'. Moreover, the humanitarian consequences of the LRA incursions into Uganda became, for the first time, a major focus of international attention. All sorts of important people suddenly wanted to visit northern Uganda, see the situation for themselves and give briefings to the international media. Most vociferous of all was Jan Egeland, the UN Under-Secretary for Humanitarian Affairs. In November 2003 he remarked that: 'The situation is intolerable and we must all agree as an international community, the UN and donors, that this is totally unacceptable. Northern Uganda is the most forgotten crisis in the world.'[1]

The pressure on the Ugandan government was then increased in January 2004 when the US Congress passed the 'Northern Uganda Crisis Response Act'.[2] This noted the point that the Sudan government was probably still supporting the LRA, making it very clear that this was unacceptable to the USA, and it called for more resources to be made available to the region for assistance programmes and protection of the population. But, significantly, it also called for improvements in the professionalism of Uganda military personnel currently stationed in the region, and for monitoring of civilian militia forces. In addition, the State Department was required to submit a report on the conflict within six months (it eventually did so in February 2005). Given the interventionist policies of the Bush administration, this development was something that had to be taken seriously by the Ugandan government.

President Museveni appears to have recognized that he had lost the political initiative. Always a pragmatist with a knack of responding effectively to developments as they unfold, he sought to head off international criticism. On the one hand, he took measures to improve UPDF military performance, and a prosecution was announced relating to army corruption in the north, implicating the president's own brother. On the other, he allowed more space for possible peace talks, and changed his attitude towards the Amnesty Act.

The Amnesty Act

Following persistent lobbying from various activists – and overcoming outright opposition from President Museveni himself – the Amnesty Act passed into Ugandan law in November 1999 and was enacted in January 2000. It provides amnesty procedures for all rebels in Uganda, not only the LRA, and initially it was groups that had been resisting the government in other parts of the country which benefited most. Former LRA veterans report that Kony himself condemned the amnesty and threatened abductees and followers with violent reprisals if they tried to accept it. He also recalled that some of the UPDA who surrendered in 1988 were subsequently killed, allegedly by the Uganda government. In any case, President Museveni had remained unwilling to accept that the act should apply to LRA commanders, and the Anti-Terrorism Act of 2002 implicitly set limits on its application.[3] Also, the Iron Fist operation in 2002 made clear that the military option was still preferred.

From 2003, however, international as well as local demands were being made to make the amnesty process more effective.

16 An amnesty card: after returning from the LRA some people are issued with documents under the Amnesty Act (Elliott Green)

In the aftermath of the first Iron Fist offensive, it proved understandably difficult to communicate with the mass of the LRA about it, or convince the LRA commanders that it was genuine. Nevertheless, the numbers of former LRA soldiers and abductees accepting the amnesty increased, with quite large numbers giving themselves up since 2003. By mid-2004, over five thousand adult former LRA fighters had surrendered and applied for it.

One reason for the uptake was that the military activities of the UPDF in Sudan had started to have more effect. Some of those with the LRA were captured or rescued, such as 'Brigadier' Kenneth Banya and some of Kony's 'wives'. Others became separated from their commanders and could escape, or were unable to access food supplies and were starved into surrender. Another reason was that there was some success in communicating with the LRA rank and file through Mega Radio, the FM station broadcast from Gulu, which can be heard very clearly in much of central northern Uganda as well as parts of southern Sudan. Individuals who had been given amnesty were taken to the radio station and interviewed about what had happened to them. They called on their friends still with the LRA to try to return home too. The LRA commanders responded by stopping their soldiers/abductees from listening to radios, but it took only one person to hear and the word was passed around. Several of the former LRA combatants I spoke to in November 2004 told me that they had heard about the amnesty in this way.

Unfortunately, it was not anticipated how Kony and his senior commanders would react to the radio broadcasts. The growing numbers of LRA fighters accepting the amnesty were understandably seen as a threat. When a handful of key commanders surrendered together with their units in May 2004, the response was dreadful. Mega Radio interviewed one of them and also transmitted a programme from Pagak, the commander's home, where there was a party to celebrate. A week later, the LRA attacked at night. They looted the camp, set the houses on fire and took around fifty people into the bush, where they clubbed or hacked most of them to death. Almost twenty were still alive in the morning, but with terrible injuries. Many were mothers and their babies. Others were young children. The UPDF soldiers who were supposed to protect them had just run away. A few days later a further revenge attack occurred at another IDP camp, Lukodi. On that occasion twenty-eight people were killed.

These events highlighted the fact that LRA commanders knew about the amnesty process, but some did not want to accept it. They indicated that it could not be a solution in itself. Also, the numbers of LRA veterans taking the amnesty declined to a trickle from late 2004. Nevertheless, there was passionate support for it in northern Uganda among political activists, churches, NGOs and an influential group of 'traditional' leaders. The local councils had also become involved, implementing by-laws that made it an offence to insult or harass returned combatants and abductees. As we shall see, there was a tendency among these groups to associate the amnesty with a more general notion of forgiveness. In fact in the Lwo language, 'amnesty' and 'forgiveness' are not distinct – the same word (*timo-kica*) is used for both. The Christian organizations and the 'traditional' leaders

17 Mothers and their children were hacked to death at Pagak in May 2004. People at the camp had welcomed 'home' a group of LRA soldiers. This was how the LRA responded.

were especially prone to confuse the two ideas, even arguing that there is an Acholi system of justice based on forgiveness which is superior to more conventional law-making and enforcement. Rather naively, many NGOs have taken this at face value.

President Museveni himself reluctantly accepted this offer of amnesty to the LRA, although he has continued to voice reservations about it applying to Kony himself and his notorious supporters. Like senior UPDF officers I interviewed at the time, he persisted in asserting the need for a military campaign. Throughout 2004 and into 2005, operations in Sudan continued. Nevertheless, the UPDF has generally been willing to protect those who return. Many have been sent to the various reception centres funded by aid agencies, such as the one run by World Vision in Gulu. Others, notably the more senior former LRA officers, have been accommodated at one of the many army barracks or allowed to settle in one of the towns. In addition, there is a policy of actively recruiting younger men into local defence forces or into the UPDF, allegedly with a degree of compulsion. A special battalion of the UPDF, the 105th, has been established specifically for this purpose. By the end of 2004, almost eight hundred had been integrated in this way (to the considerable unease of UNICEF and other agencies, because many had participated in atrocities and some were thought to be under-age for recruitment). A concern being voiced by some local informants at the time was that the 105th might be deployed against their former colleagues in the LRA if the current peace talks broke down. That is currently the case, although they are not acting as a cohesive unit. Small groups from the 105th are deployed to work with other battalions, mainly to assist with intelligence (such as the targeting of collaborators and the location of arms stocks).

Peace talks

There had been various attempts at negotiation since Betty Bigombe's efforts in 1994, but none of them had come to much. A group called the Acholi Religious Leaders Peace Initiative (ARLPI) was established in 1998, and in addition to lobbying for the Amnesty Act it managed to keep a window of communication open with the LRA. These links had on occasion indicated the possibility of negotiations, but neither the LRA nor the Ugandan government had really been committed to making them work. In April 2003 the LRA broke a ceasefire that it had declared unilaterally when it killed a representative of a Presidential peace team. Since then, there has seemed little prospect of talks. Kony and his commanders had occasionally used mobile phones to ring certain peace activists (notably some Catholic priests), but the Ugandan government had sometimes viewed this with hostility, making accusations of collaboration with the rebels.

Nevertheless, the ARLPI and other activists kept trying to push for more talks, and in May 2004 Betty Bigombe, who had been working in Washington for the World Bank, was asked to act as a peace envoy. She travelled to Sudan with aid donor funding, and tried to make contact with Kony from Juba. The Sudan government ensured, however, that meetings did not take place. Here is an exchange with a young LRA soldier who had originally been abducted from a primary school. He had escaped and accepted the amnesty just before the interview, which took place in the World Vision reception centre in Gulu in November 2004. He comments on Bigombe's attempts to contact Kony:

Does Kony want to be peaceful sometimes?

Yes, I think he has the will to behave peacefully but the evil spirits in him would make him appear violent most of the time.

Do you think if Kony was offered a good deal he would come out and make peace?

Kony fears to come by himself so he would rather send his representative because he says that he knows what the government's intentions are ... To him the only peace talks that could have succeeded were those of 1994, but the rest did not hold water. He cited for us an example of the 2002 peace deal which turned futile. He claims he was given restricted areas of Pajok, Owinykibul and Palutaka from where he could meet the mediators and talk peace. He added that all these places are in the Sudan and yet the peace was being talked for Uganda. According to him, this didn't make sense. Even after endeavouring to assemble in the said areas, the government troops breeched the agreement and attacked his troops. And it's true we were attacked but we defeated the government troops.

Do you think Kony would be willing to meet Betty Bigombe again?

Yes, because he says Bigombe is a true child of Acholi ...

Bigombe was in Juba but failed to meet Kony. What do you say about that?

But we were not informed about her presence in Sudan.

Do you think it was the government of Sudan which prevented it?

Yes, I think so because we were in Sudan around April and May if that was the time that Bigombe was there.

When I spoke to her on the phone in October 2004, Bigombe was pessimistic that anything could be achieved north of the

79

border. One senior LRA commander, Sam Kolo, had wanted to link up with her in Sudan, and there seemed a chance that contact might be possible from northern Uganda. Several aid donors were interested in this possibility, including the UK and the USA – which has recently started funding something called the Northern Uganda Peace Initiative (NUPI). Bigombe went to Gulu in November and with President Museveni's permission entered into negotiations, which quickly led to the setting up of a limited ceasefire zone close to the border with Sudan, to the east of Atiak.

It was an uneasy affair, and there continued to be violent incidents outside the gazetted area. Kony himself showed no sign of moving into the zone and, according to UPDF intelligence, ordered his commanders to leave Uganda and rejoin him in Sudan. At least one effort was made to target him in ongoing UPDF attacks on LRA positions north of the border. Nevertheless, Betty Bigombe and her team managed to build up a degree of trust with Sam Kolo, and held some meetings. International observers, including a British army officer, accompanied her. She herself thought that there was a real possibility that at least some of the LRA would agree to terms, and used her influence with President Museveni to keep the ceasefire zone after its allotted expiry date.

On the face of it, a ceasefire zone and peace talks should have been unnecessary, because the amnesty appears to guarantee impunity. The arrangements had important purposes, however. First, they were a means of persuading the LRA that they would not be punished if they surrendered. Second, they offered an alternative way for the LRA commanders to agree to stop the killing, even if they do not want to simply accept the terms of the amnesty. It was clear that there were commanders in the LRA who did not want 'forgiveness', which implies an admission of guilt, so much as a negotiated settlement. Basically, they wanted to be taken seriously and not dismissed as lunatics or misguided children. Even if they had set aside any specific political demands, they wanted both impunity and some kind of secure livelihood. There was also a third reason why the talks may have been valuable for the LRA, one that UPDF officers were prone to point out. The ceasefire gave the LRA a dry-season breathing space after the renewed Iron Fist operations in Sudan. It could be that they were just biding their time, and had no real intention of making peace. President Museveni himself remained openly sceptical about negotiations.

Nevertheless, he agreed to extensions of the ceasefire, initially on a week-by-week basis. Outside the gazetted area, the LRA launched small-scale attacks and several rebels were killed in exchanges with the UPDF. One of these occurred just outside Atiak while I was researching in the camp in November 2004. In early December the size of the ceasefire zone was reduced and active operations against the LRA were resumed elsewhere in northern Uganda. But the ceasefire zone was extended to Sudan for a few days in the middle of the month, apparently to allow Kony to meet his second-in-command, Vincent Otti.[4] A ceasefire arrangement was still in place in early 2005 and in February was extended again when Kolo's colleague, 'Colonel' Onen Kamdulu, surrendered. Kamdulu announced that Kony was still in Sudan but ready to make a deal. The talks then ran into problems, however.

In mid-February 'Brigadier' Sam Kolo himself had to be evacuated by the UPDF when he refused to obey a command from Kony to return to Sudan. After that there was no senior commander to negotiate with, and the ceasefire zone was reoccupied by the UPDF. Towards the end of the month and in March there were more reported LRA mutilations and killings, including several in Adjumani district, and some small-scale engagements with the UPDF. Similar incidents have continued intermittently. In

April the UPDF commenced an offensive in southern Sudan, and the LRA retaliated with several attacks in Uganda, including more mutilations. In May the UPDF killed an LRA 'brigadier' who had attended meetings in the bush between Kolo and Bigombe. Bigombe herself left for the USA for a period, but has returned. At the time of writing (in early August 2005) she is still trying to keep the door to talks open. Messages are going out on Mega Radio giving a radio frequency and calling on the LRA leaders to make contact. Bigombe has been waiting in the UN office each morning for a reply. So far there has been no response from Kony, although Otti has rung Bigombe's mobile phone saying he wants to meet. Perhaps they will, but expectations of a comprehensive peace deal have receded.

Referral to the ICC

It was in this environment of fragile peace talks and amnesty arrangements that the ICC intervened. The referral had been made at the end of 2003, but was not announced until January 2004 by President Museveni and Chief Prosecutor Moreno-Ocampo together at a briefing in London. The press statement that followed noted that: ' ... the Ugandan authorities have enacted an amnesty law. President Museveni has indicated to the Prosecutor his intention to amend this amnesty so as to exclude the leadership of the LRA, ensuring that those bearing the greatest responsibility for the crimes against humanity committed in Northern Uganda are brought to justice'.[5]

The Office of the Prosecutor then commenced initial enquiries. The ICC had much to prove, and open antipathy from the USA to overcome. Doubtless 'the situation concerning the Lord's Resistance Army' seemed like a relatively simple case to start with, one that would help to establish the court's credentials. The suggestion that the ICC should prosecute the LRA had in fact been made by UNICEF in New York back in 1998, four years before the ratification of the Rome Treaty, and when the intervention become public several aid agencies and human rights organizations expressed enthusiasm, seeing it as something of breakthrough. Amnesty International hailed it as 'first steps', which should be 'part a comprehensive plan to end impunity'.[6] So staff from the court had expectations of a relatively positive reaction from activists and organizations working on the ground. That this was not the case took them by surprise. Both the complexities of the war and the responses of those trying to end it by peaceful means presented the court with unforeseen difficulties.

Reactions to the ICC in Uganda

Soon after the ICC intervention was announced, a group of UNICEF staff from New York travelled to Uganda with the intention of briefing colleagues about the good news. They received a frosty reaction. The concerns of field-based staff were similar to those expressed by Save the Children in Uganda (SCiU) in a public statement issued in February 2004. Among other points, this drew attention to serious doubts about the timing of the investigation, and about how the possible arrest and prosecution of the LRA leadership will affect the rights of the children still in captivity, as well as the rights of all children in northern Uganda.

> We have to realize that this war primarily involves children, thus any action taken must seriously consider the impact on child protection ... Children are by far the main witnesses (and victims) ... Save the Children is concerned that the LRA leadership might apply even more strict discipline to prevent witnesses from escaping. They could also easily convince the children that they will be subject to prosecution by the ICC if they do so. In other words, their hold and control over the child hostages can be increased, as well as the risks to children associated with

escaping from the LRA. This is likely to prevent more children from escaping including newly abducted ones ... It can be assumed that the lives of those children who have managed to return from abduction will be endangered, especially if they give evidence to the ICC. This may also have implications for the present practices of rehabilitation and reintegration, where organizations working in this field actively encourage children to return to their communities following assessment and assistance in the rehabilitation centres. Who will be held accountable for the safety and protection of these children? ... In general we find that it is extremely challenging to impart clear information to war-torn communities in ways that will be properly understood by the majority and not converted into damaging rumours, leading to even more suspicion and distrust.[7]

The Save the Children statement also noted that attempts to arrest the LRA leadership in the absence of any peace agreement may translate into, even justify, an increased military offensive by the government of Uganda, which the LRA are likely to respond to with more violence against citizens. This view was echoed by many others in Uganda, who were deeply sceptical of President Museveni's motives, seeing it as no more than a political manoeuvre – a mechanism to reassert his international credentials after the failure of the 2002 Iron Fist offensive, put pressure on the government of Sudan and deflect attention from Ugandan activities in eastern Congo.[8] The government's own Amnesty Commission expressed fears that the announcement by the ICC could make a peaceful resolution of the eighteen-year conflict impossible.[9]

The Save the Children statement had called for a thorough risk assessment before the ICC went any farther, and the agency had discussions with the court about how this might be done. It was not carried out, however (or rather the ICC decided that

18 Save the Children has understandably drawn attention to the rights and needs of children. Concerns have been raised about how those living in the IDP camps will be protected from LRA attacks once ICC warrants are issued (Elliott Green)

it could not be delegated to a third party and did it internally), and following the appalling LRA attacks of February to May 2004, Moreno-Ocampo wrote to the president of the court on 17 June, stating that there was sufficient evidence to proceed with an investigation. State parties were notified on 21 June, and the decision was announced in Uganda on 28 July. It made local actors feel that their voices had simply been ignored, and some made no effort to hide their anger, particularly when the amnesty and peace talks showed signs of producing results later in the year.

The vice-president of the ARLPI, retired Anglican Bishop Baker Ochola, is reported to have told a UN reporter, 'This kind of approach is going to destroy all efforts for peace. People want this war to stop. If we follow the ICC in branding the LRA criminals, it won't stop.' Perhaps the most prominent and widely respected ARLPI activist, Father Carlos Rodriguez, made the following public statement:

> The issuing of ... international arrest warrants would practically close once and for all the path to peaceful negotiation as a means to end this long war, crushing whatever little progress has been made during these years ... Obviously, nobody can convince the leaders of a rebel movement to come to the negotiating table

85

and at the same time tell them that they will appear in courts to be prosecuted.[10]

With respect to the president's proposed amendments to the Amnesty Act to exclude Kony and his senior commanders, an Amnesty Commission spokesperson stated that it 'is going to make it very difficult for the LRA to stop doing what they are doing'. Those calling for forgiveness in the broad sense went so far as to assert that the ICC reflected flawed and compromised systems of justice, and that it could not comprehend the meaning of the real justice known to the Acholi, grounded in what are asserted to be traditional or Christian values. I discussed this latter view with retired Bishop Ochola in November 2004. He suspected that I must have some connection with the ICC and could barely contain himself. He lectured me for over an hour about what he saw as local understandings and accused the ICC of trying to make a name for itself out of the suffering of his people – and, indeed, his own suffering: his wife had been killed by an LRA landmine.

In November, ARLPI and the Acholi Paramount Chief Elect made the following joint statement to Chief Prosecutor Moreno-Ocampo.[11]

> The ICC should write to both the LRA and government of Uganda stating clearly its intention to halt any further investigation and prosecution and express its commitments to support the on-going peace process. This will be a concrete step in building confidence and trust on both sides. While we recognize your need to investigate into the crimes committed by the LRA against humanity, we would strongly suggest that the investigation encompasses the whole situation of the war in northern Uganda in order for true justice to be done ... We reiterate that the Amnesty Law and Dialogue options are the most relevant solution that befits our current situation. Therefore, the ICC intervention at

this particular moment sends conflicting signals to the on-going peace process and could easily jeopardize its success.

Even Ugandan human rights groups opposed the intervention. When I interviewed James Otto, the head of the Gulu-based Human Rights Watch, in early March 2005, he was incandescent about the court (he spoke to me in English).

> The ICC timing is bad. It has no protection mechanism. We have our own traditional justice system. The international system despises it, but it works. There is a balance in the community that cannot be found in the briefcase of the white man. Old values regulate our lives and they are still cherished. There is a view that the West has nothing to learn. They have brought the death penalty and incorporated it in our law. But we did not have it before. The real issue for the ICC is that the USA is out of its yoke. It should deal with that and leave us alone. The problems here can be traditionally handled. The ICC see Uganda as a soft target. If we had the military might of the USA we would be talking to the ICC on equal terms. We are forced to kneel. Where is the justice in that? What is good for the goose should be good for the gander. We told Ocampo [i.e. the Chief Prosecutor] what the political connotations are. But it seems that justice is just there to be meted out on the weak by the strong. Do they want to keep this war going for perpetuity?

Such antipathy in Uganda from the very organizations that it hoped to work with on the ground has placed the ICC in a difficult position. As a matter of policy, the Office of the Prosecutor makes no comments on specific ongoing investigative activities, partly for reasons of witness security. Attempts have been made to interact with a range of partners, including community leaders and relevant international organizations. These activities, however, have mostly been low key and/or confidential, and those parts of the ICC, notably the Registry, that should at some point play an active role in promoting public awareness of the legal proceedings have been largely inactive.[12] Staff at the ICC are aware that they have to tread carefully. It would not help the new institution if the violence in the region escalated and the ICC were held to be responsible. Moreover, the Rome Statute requires the ICC to act in the interests of justice and the interest of victims – although exactly what this means in practice is not clear. A consequence of the ICC approach is that knowledge about its role in northern Uganda is very limited. Even senior UPDF commanders I interviewed in November 2004 were confused. They thought that the ICC was the ICJ, and would be dealing with the problem as a border dispute between Uganda and Sudan. What is known about the ICC mostly comes from occasional statements in the national media, many of which are misleading, and the 'damaging rumours' highlighted in the SCiU statement are prevalent. The impression has been given that the ICC is secretive. This leads to speculation about what it might or might not do. In the next chapter I explore concerns that have been raised about the intervention in detail. But first it is necessary to outline some of the specific legal aspects of the intervention.

Legal aspects of the ICC intervention

The Rome Statute and the capacities of the ICC have already been outlined in Chapter 1. Here I reiterate some of those points with specific reference to the Ugandan intervention.

1 Of the four kinds of crime mentioned in the ICC statute, in the Ugandan case prosecutions have been prepared for crimes against humanity and war crimes. It is likely that warrants will make reference to both kinds of crime. Somewhat confusingly, it is possible for both crimes to be committed simultaneously, because of overlapping definitions.

2 The ICC will not seek to prosecute everyone who is alleged to have committed crimes, but only individuals who are thought to be most responsible for committing the most serious crimes falling within the jurisdiction of the court. Following the models of the ICTY, ICTR and SCSL, in Uganda the ICC prosecutor is likely to have prepared warrants for fewer than ten individuals. It should be noted that those for whom warrants are issued may or may not be senior LRA commanders who have refused to accept amnesty or peace terms. The prosecutor could, for example, choose to prosecute Kenneth Banya, a former LRA commander who has accepted the amnesty. It may be that the ICC will avoid doing this, but it does not have to do so. The ICC does not even have to recognize Ugandan presidential immunity.

3 Successful prosecution will require that a clear pattern of crimes and a clear line of command be established. It will not be enough to demonstrate that crimes against humanity or war crimes have occurred. This may mean that some of the worst crimes will not be cited. The Office of the Prosecutor is likely to concentrate on those serious crimes for which it is likely that conviction of an individual can be secured.

4 The ICTY, the ICTR and the SCSL can investigate only alleged crimes that occurred within specific time frames and in those specific territories.[13] The ICC, in contrast, may investigate alleged crimes that have taken place in the territory of any member state or by the national of any member state since its formal inception in July 2002. This is a reason why the USA is so hostile to the ICC, while it has been one of the main funders of the other institutions: the jurisdiction of the ICTY, ICTR and the SCSL do not directly compromise US sovereignty.

5 An implication of the US opposition to the ICC is that the UN Security Council has been unable to support it. In a recent request by the government of Burundi to the ICC (relating to the massacre of 150 Congolese refugees in Gatumba on 13 August

2004), the USA refused to support a Security Council resolution renewing the mandate of the UN mission in Burundi until wording endorsing Burundi's request to the ICC was removed. The resolution was adopted on 2 December 2004 without explicit reference to the ICC.[14] This kind of pressure leaves the ICC dependent on member governments for logistical support, which could undermine the independence of the court – an accusation that has already been made in the Ugandan case.

6 An important difference between the ICC and the ICTR and ICTY is that it is not the creation of the UN Security Council. Like the SCSL, the ICC is based on the consent of states formalized in an agreement. The authority of the ICC changes if there is a Security Council referral, otherwise the ICC is similar to the SCSL in that it does not have the enforcement powers under Chapter VII of the UN Charter. In other words, the ICC has to rely on its member states to cooperate. There is considerable misunderstanding about this in Uganda, even among senior army officers. In Sierra Leone, the problem was partially dealt with by a Special Court Act, making the SCSL's decisions directly executable on Sierra Leone territory (but not in neighbouring Liberia). The presence of British troops on the ground also helped facilitate a situation in which the SCSL was accorded authority and respect. The current position of the ICC in Uganda is more precarious. There are no peacekeeping forces, and the court's statute has not yet been implemented in Ugandan law, potentially making its work on the ground difficult. The ICC is not bound by amnesty or immunity arrangements (including presidential immunity). In Ugandan law, however, the ICC's authority appears to be in conflcit with, among other things, the Amnesty Act – although this may change if the Amnesty Act lapses or is amended. More generally, until the ICC statute becomes part of Ugandan law, it is not clear that the Ugandan police (or army) would be able to execute an ICC arrest warrant.[15]

7 Without Security Council support, the ICC cannot avoid having a close relationship with the governments of state parties. Article 1 of the statute explains that the ICC is 'complementary to national criminal jurisdictions'. It is on this basis that it has been asked to intervene in northern Uganda by President Museveni. It means that the ICC has been requested to deal with crimes that are beyond the capacities of the Ugandan judicial system. In a sense, it is filling a gap and acting on behalf of the Ugandan state, even though the Ugandan government is itself involved in the conflict. The ICC had apparently been quietly analysing the situation in northern Uganda before the referral,[16] and might have launched an investigation even if the referral had not occurred. The fact that it did occur provides the court with more powers (because of the way it operates with the assistance of state parties).[17] But in this instance it has certainly created an awkward impression.

8 Individuals for whom warrants are likely to be issued are currently in Sudan, and it is not clear what the status of ICC warrants will be on Sudanese territory. Like the USA, Sudan has signed, but not ratified the ICC Rome Statute. Under the Vienna Convention on the Law of Treaties (1969),[18] Sudan is bound to refrain from 'acts which would defeat the objective and purpose' of the statute, and the statute provides that any warrants issued by the court will be transmitted to those states in which the suspect is believed to be present. Thus, the government of Sudan may be compelled to cooperate by international pressure. During 2004, the ICC negotiated a bilateral agreement with the government of Sudan, which indicated publicly that it would cooperate in arresting and surrendering suspects sought by the ICC. The Office of the Prosecutor also discussed the necessary legal arrangements to ensure cooperation in the interests of making warrants effective. The Sudan government never actually implemented the agreement, however, and withdrew cooperation

once there was a possibility of the situation in Darfur being referred to the court in January 2005.[19] If warrants are issued for LRA commanders, the Sudan government might adopt the same position as the government of Nigeria has done with respect to the SCSL warrant for Charles Taylor. In the Ugandan case this could be even more damaging. If those wanted by the ICC are not arrested in a relatively short space of time, everyone concerned with promoting peace in northern Uganda will have an interest in subverting the warrants.

9 The ICC has launched an investigation in Uganda while fighting is continuing. It may be that there was an expectation that the war was more or less over in late 2003. That was, after all, what the government was claiming. Also, it was probably anticipated that the peace process in Sudan would incapacitate the LRA by closing off its line of support. The war has not stopped, however, and it has been argued that this sets the ICC intervention apart from that of the ICTR, the ICTY and the SCSL. As the title of one recent report on the ICC's role in Uganda (and the Congo) puts it, the court is moving 'in uncharted waters', because it is 'seeking justice before the atrocities have stopped'.[20] Actually this is not completely accurate. The ICTY was launched in the thick of hostilities, and its mandate was ongoing throughout the fighting in Kosovo. Nevertheless, there were serious prospects of an international intervention to impose order. That was not an imminent prospect in Uganda during 2004, and at the time of writing, in mid-2005, a comprehensive peace settlement is far from certain.

10 In Sierra Leone, the SCSL had a regime for the conduct of proceedings against fifteen-to-eighteen-year-olds – an issue of much concern for child protection agencies (although no children have actually been prosecuted). The ICC, however, is much more favourable towards children. Article 26 explicitly states that the court shall have no jurisdiction over any person who was

under the age of eighteen at the time of the alleged commission of a crime. This does not preclude prosecution of someone who was abducted as a child but was over eighteen at the time when alleged crimes were committed. There are many who might fit into this category in northern Uganda. It is likely, however, that the court will want to avoid controversy over the issue.

11 Even when crimes within the jurisdiction of the ICC have occurred, under Article 53 of the Rome Statute, the prosecutor can decide that to proceed with a prosecution is 'not in the interests of justice taking into account all the circumstances, including the gravity of the crime, the interests of victims and the age or infirmity of the alleged perpetrator, and his or her role in the alleged crime'. The chief prosecutor would then have to present a case to the ICC's Pre-Trial Chamber. If his argument is accepted, the case will be dropped. When I discussed this possibility with staff at the ICC Office of the Prosecutor in The Hague in January 2005, they were adamant that it was extremely unlikely. More recently they have been a little more equivocal.[21] In April 2005, the chief prosecutor was reported to have said that 'as soon as there is a solution to end the violence and if the prosecution is not serving the interests of justice, then my duty is to stop investigation and prosecution. I will stop but I will not close. Timing is possible but immunity is not possible.'[22]

12 Once arrests have been made, a criminal trial will take place at the seat of the court, unless it is 'otherwise decided'. Thus it is possible that trials could take place in Uganda. A case could be made for doing this, drawing on the model of the SCSL. Otherwise the trials will be in The Hague – and this seems more likely, given the security and cost implications of a Ugandan location. It is important to note that trial *in absentia* is not possible according to the Rome Statute. The accused must be present during the trial, unless he or she is removed for disrupting proceedings.

13 The accused will be given ample time and resources to prepare a defence. The defence will not be constrained by the July 2002 date (i.e. the defence will be able to refer to events that occurred before this date). This may not prove to be significant because the defence should be a direct response to the accusations that have been made. Moreover, the ICC will be eager to avoid the kind of open-ended proceedings that have occurred at the ICTY and ICTR, so counsel will be directed to keep to the point. If the LRA commanders decide to present their own defence, however, they will have to be given latitude by the judge. This could prove to be politically embarrassing for the Ugandan government.

It seems unlikely that President Museveni himself knew all this when he invited Chief Prosecutor Luis Moreno-Ocampo to become involved. Now that some of the implications of a referral to the ICC are apparent, he seems to have had second thoughts. He has said that if Bigombe's negotiations are successful, he will ask the ICC to stop its investigation.[23] He is not actually in a position to stop proceedings (he can try to persuade the Office of the Prosecutor to make a case to the Pre-Trial Chamber that to proceed would not be in the interests of justice and/or victims). He could certainly make things very difficult for the court, however, if he withdrew his government's active cooperation.

Faced with a barrage of antipathy from unexpected sources, and then with equivocation about prosecutions of the LRA from Uganda's president, the ICC mainly responded with public silence. This was in marked contrast to what seemed to be a rather open attitude soon after the referral was made – reflected in the January 2004 press conference in London.

The following chapters address directly key concerns that have been raised about the ICC intervention. These have been expressed very clearly in a range of reports, articles and public statements, notably the SCiU statement, the Refugee Law Project position paper, the report by the Citizens for Global Solutions, the transcript of the ICC discussion meeting held in Gulu in August 2004, and in the excellent articles by Barney Afako and Adam Branch.[24] Owing to the paucity of information about the ICC in northern Uganda, concerns have mostly been expressed by activists and analysts rather than local people themselves. Nevertheless, the same issues are often raised in interviews and discussions when the activities, powers and limitations of the court are explained. There are, in addition, certain perspectives and worries that do not appear in the wider public discourse. These relate to experiences and interpretations of the violence grounded in local understandings, including understandings of Kony's power and influence.

5 | Concerns about the court

Essentially the main concerns about the ICC intervention in Uganda are the following: it is biased; it will exacerbate the violence; it will endanger vulnerable groups – notably witnesses and children; it is spoiling the peace process by undermining the amnesty and the ceasefire; and it ignores and disempowers local justice procedures. The concerns obviously overlap one another. For clarity, however, it will be appropriate to treat them under separate sub-headings. In each case I provide a discussion of the issues raised and end with a brief assessment of the evidence. The last-mentioned concern about local justice processes takes us beyond the current controversies about the ICC to an engagement with the wider possibilities of social healing. It is dealt with separately in Chapter 6.

The ICC is biased

The impression that the ICC intervention in Uganda is biased was given right at the start by the fact that Chief Prosecutor Moreno-Ocampo and President Museveni held a joint press briefing in January 2004, announcing that the ICC would begin preliminary investigations. Even Amnesty International, which welcomed the announcement, chose to make the point that 'Any Court investigation of war crimes and crimes against humanity in northern Uganda must be part of a comprehensive plan to end impunity for all such crimes, regardless of which side committed them and the level of the perpetrator.'[1] The implication was clear: the court should also consider prosecution of people associated with the Ugandan government, something that it is empowered to do by the Rome Statute. In response to this and other statements from human rights and development agencies, the Chief Prosecutor clarified his office's position in February, and reiterated it in a formal letter to the President of the Court on 17 June 2004: 'My Office has informed the Ugandan authorities that we must interpret the scope of the referral consistently with the principles of the Rome Statute, and hence we are analysing crimes within the situation of northern Uganda by whomever committed.'[2]

This clarification has done little, however, to challenge the view that the Office of the Prosecutor is acting on behalf of President Museveni, and will not attempt to punish the UPDF as well as the LRA. There are several reasons for this. As Adam Branch points out, alleged UPDF abuses have been public knowledge for years, with no adverse effect for the Ugandan government. On the contrary, 'essential US support for the Ugandan military has increased to include, since September 11, 2001, funds earmarked to eliminate LRA "Terrorists"'.[3] It also seems unlikely that President Museveni would have initiated the prosecution if he thought he could not control it. Technically he may be wrong when he claims that he can stop the ICC proceedings if he no longer deems them necessary, but if he actively opposed prosecutions it would make them very difficult. Some legal analysts have additionally noted that serious complications could arise from an attempt to prosecute both sides, in that arguments presented by the prosecution in one case might form part of the defence in another (and vice versa).[4]

The biased nature of the ICC's intervention also seems to be indicated by rumours about the investigators' use of Ugandan government vehicles and officials to facilitate their enquiries on the ground,[5] and by the lack of information about what the court has been doing since mid-2004, when the formal investigation by the Office of the Prosecutor began. The latter has given the impression that the ICC has things to hide over and above the

97

obvious need for confidentiality in preparing warrants. It also means that the initial press releases about the referral have been given more weight than was probably intended. They are still the first things that come up about Uganda on the ICC website, and the chief prosecutor's subsequent clarification is often ignored or dismissed. There have been no significant efforts by the ICC Registry to counter these perceptions or promote awareness and understanding of what the court is supposed to be doing in Uganda. As a result, most of those who have tried to follow events closely are sceptical about Chief Prosecutor Moreno-Ocampo's claims to objectivity, and anticipate that warrants will be issued only for Kony and a handful of his top commanders. While there is widespread acceptance that these people are responsible for appalling acts, several commentators take the view that to focus on them alone cannot lead to a just outcome.

Here are a few quotes illustrating this concern about objectivity. The first is from Barney Afako of Justice Resources. He is one of the leading legal analysts of the ICC investigation. His comments are taken from the transcript of the ICC discussion meeting held in Gulu on 13 August 2004.

> The Prosecutor has to prioritise ... His prioritisation is to go after a few people, but only those who are most responsible ... Also I suspect that he will ... go for the most serious crimes. I would be surprised if he sought to prosecute more than about five people ... The UPDF is unlikely to be prosecuted ... because of the difficulty of making the charges stick ...

The second quote is from an interview with the outspoken retired bishop Baker Ochola, vice-president of ARLPI, interviewed in English in November 2004.

> The ICC will not be a solution. We want the whole story to be told ... If they just investigate the LRA, it will be an injustice to

society ... The ICC cannot impose itself on people. The government is inviting it, so it has already lost its impartiality. It is an injustice ... We have not invited it. They are already biased. It is an abuse ... The ICC is just full of corruption ... The government has killed. They have all killed. The LRA has done bad things, so has the government. We need to investigate everything ... The ICC is an enticement for individuals to oppose individuals ...

The next quote comes from Onan Acana, the Paramount Chief Elect (he was crowned on 17 January 2005). It is taken from an interview in English, also in November 2004.

How can the ICC be impartial if it is only working on one side of the conflict? There should be justice, administered impartially ... We have had soldiers raping men. We have had people thrown in pits ... Where government soldiers have committed crimes, should we just ignore it? The ICC says that if the government atrocities are as bad as LRA atrocities they will investigate. I will wait and see ...

Longer extracts from the interviews with Onan Acana and Baker Ochola are discussed below. They have been among the most important advocates of forgiveness instead of punishment, so they have a particular reason for questioning the integrity of the court. Most of those I have spoken to in the IDP camps did not know enough about the ICC to comment on the issue. Several noted, however, that the Ugandan government forces should also be investigated. For example, one local council officer told me that 'There are also notorious commanders on the government side. They also committed inhumane acts ... '; and a former LRA combatant remarked that 'The current government was also abducting people to fight for them during the previous war. Why can't the ICC allow the community to give testimonies, because some people were abducted by the government to become soldiers?'

Assessment of the evidence: is the ICC biased? The unwillingness of the ICC to explain what it is doing makes it hard to counter these various accusations of bias. To a large extent, however, they are a consequence of the way states party referals work under the Rome Statute. The ICC does not have the same primacy of jurisdiction enjoyed by the Hague Tribunal. The joint press briefing in London was obviously a serious error of judgement. It is quite possible, however, that the Office of the Prosecutor has been operating quietly and the Registry has been largely inactive in order to give time for the amnesty and current peace negotiations to run their course.[6] Also, the Rome Statute has not yet been incorporated into Ugandan law, and the proposed changes in the Amnesty Act have not yet been implemented. So it may have been decided to move more slowly and carefully than originally anticipated.

It is possible, too, that a prosecution of the UPDF is being considered. Office of the Prosecutor staff are understandably vague about this, but do not rule it out. One senior Dutch civil servant, who seemed to be in a position to know, told me in May 2005 that at least one warrant had been prepared. The ICC's press release of January 2004, giving background information on the situation in Uganda, mentions both conscription of children and forced displacement of civilians as possible 'crimes against humanity'.[7] The UPDF is alleged to have performed both of these acts. Also, some legal analysts take the view that prosecution of individuals in both the LRA and the UPDF at the same time is feasible, provided cases are discrete, and when asked about this, staff at the ICC were surprised that it had been raised as an issue. Nevertheless, a successful prosecution of a government official or UPDF officer would be very difficult.

Apart from the likely lack of cooperation from the Ugandan government, it will be easier to establish a pattern of serious crimes committed at the behest of LRA commanders than it would be for the UPDF. Also, the Office of the Prosecutor would proceed with a prosecution only if the alleged crime was manifestly of great gravity. It would be hard to make such a case, partly because the defence would be able to demonstrate that massacres of civilians by the LRA have occurred and could therefore argue that the government of Uganda and the UPDF had a duty to remove people from danger, even if they did not perceive it as being in their interests. For these reasons, it will be a surprise if warrants are actually served for individuals who are not members of the LRA.

Given these limitations, the argument that the ICC in Uganda is fundamentally compromised is an overstatement. The Office of the Prosecutor should be independent, but once an investigation has begun, a case has to be made for warrants and eventually an argument presented in court with the intention of securing convictions. In this sense, any prosecutor is supposed to be biased. It is how the system works. The accused and his or her counsel will also have time to prepare a defence. In the case of the ICC this will be fully funded and presented in open court. This may lead to a kind of creeping truth commission emerging through the proceedings. It is also possible that a formal truth commission could be set up independently of the court, excluding from impunity only those who are to be prosecuted. Sierra Leone offers a model of such a procedure – although one that is far from ideal.[8]

There is one further point that needs to be made here, one that has not been highlighted in the various discussions about the ICC investigation and was raised only implicitly by a couple of my informants. The LRA is closely associated with the Acholi and most of those who have suffered the consequences of the war are Acholi. The LRA has also perpetrated atrocities among the neighbouring Madi, Langi and Teso, however, and these events have been concentrated in the period since the Rome Treaty was ratified (i.e. after mid-2002). Among Madi people in Adjumani district and to a lesser extent among Langi people in Lira district, I have found an interest in punishment and compensation with an ethnic/tribal aspect. It is likely that the ICC would find people among these populations who would willingly agree to testify in court, partly because they will have less fear of informants and reprisals, and also because they will not be required to accuse their own people. If this happens, there is a danger that the court proceedings could end up being effectively biased against the Acholi as a group, based on long-standing ethnic/tribal divisions. The chair of the local council in Atiak, located near the border with Adjumani district, seemed to have this in mind when he described the ways in which people speaking Lwo are now sometimes persecuted or even killed by groups of Madi (one man was stoned to death).[9] There is pressure on the ICC to secure a quick conviction, so there may be a temptation to use non-Acholi witnesses. But if the process exacerbates ethnic tension, it could be very counter-productive in political terms, whatever its merits as a legal process.

The ICC exacerbates the violence and endangers vulnerable groups

Various arguments have been put forward to suggest that the ICC intervention will have the effect of exacerbating the violence. They are premised on the view that the situation in northern Uganda is an ongoing war rather than the result of limited criminality – as has persistently been claimed by the Ugandan government. Some commentators have gone so far as to suggest that the invitation to the court to begin an investigation was aimed at justifying a concerted military response and securing international support. They argue that, because the ICC has no means of enforcing its warrants other than through the cooperation of state parties to the Rome Statute, the UPDF would in effect be given a free hand to pursue its military objectives through the pursuance of executing the warrants. According to Adam Branch: 'The execution of the arrest warrants would require a dramatic intensification of the government's counterinsurgency in order to capture the LRA leaders. The powerful minority within the government that opposes dialogue with the rebels would find their case for a "military solution" greatly strengthened by support from the international community.'[10]

There is concern that such support will extend to the Ugandan military operations in southern Sudan, which have reportedly been ferocious – killing many abducted people including children – and which have barely been monitored by international agencies. This worry seems to lie behind Barney Afako's observation that 'There will remain suspicion that the government which has always strained to increase its defence spending wished to strengthen its arguments by citing the ICC investigation and possible indictment. In a clear coup for the President, the prosecutor has publicly invited others to assist the Government of Uganda in this regard.'[11]

SCiU, the Refugee Law Project and others have also raised the issue of protection for the IDP camps. In the past the UPDF has not been able or willing to prevent raids on soft targets. Even with the recent attacks on LRA bases in Sudan and the spate of rebels accepting the amnesty, abductions and attacks have continued. Indeed, most of the senior LRA commanders remain at large, some of them operating more or less independently. It is well known that the LRA has perpetrated massacres in revenge for defections or for what is viewed as collaboration with the Ugandan government, for example at Pagak. If warrants are issued for the arrest of Kony and some of his officers, it is anticipated that they will never be willing to make peace and will assert their power in the most brutal ways imaginable.

These worries were reiterated and elaborated in interviews

103

with people in IDP camps and reception centres. Below is a selection of extracts. The first is from a conversation with an ex-LRA soldier who had been abducted from school in the early 1990s, and had been blinded in an attack. Despite not being able to see, he had escaped in August 2004, and was being cared for at the World Vision reception centre.

Have you ever heard about ICC?

Yes ... When I was already at the reception centre.

What do you think about it?

The ICC is going to give fear to many commanders who are willing to come back ...

If the community is to testify against the rebels, do you think the rebels will take revenge?

Yes, they will take revenge not only to those who will testify but on anybody, whether you testify or not, they will just take action.

Is that what they always did?

Yes. I have seen that the war is a sort of revenge, because the rebels are fighting civilians not soldiers. So when they hear about the court it will be bad.

The next exchange is taken from a group interview at Awere IDP camp. The replies are from a man whose responses echoed those of others at the meeting.

Have you ever heard about ICC?

No, but I can give my view. The ICC is going to make the war continue because those commanders who will be willing to come back will be discouraged and continue fighting. The ICC should first wait for the war to end and later they can come in and take the person who started it. He should be prosecuted ...

If you are asked to be a witness by the ICC, would you accept?

No ... Kony will come and kill everybody in this camp just because I testified against him.

104

[Here a woman added] The ICC should first wait. If they do not, it will cause fear in those who are still in the bush. They will not come back and war will just continue.

A woman who had been abducted in 1992 when she was fifteen made the following statement. She had been given as a 'wife' to one of the LRA commanders and had eventually managed to escape with her two children. She is now living in Gulu town. She knows what Kony is like from first-hand experience.

Have you ever heard about ICC?

Yes, over the radio, but I was not really happy about it, because when I was in the bush Kony could just make abrupt decisions. Sometimes they called ten people and slaughtered them just for nothing. So if he hears about the court before implementation [i.e. he is arrested] he can decide to kill everybody that is with him and he himself. That would be great loss because there are many children there.

Here are some responses from other young women, interviewed at the GUSCO reception centre in Gulu.

Do you have any knowledge about the ICC?

No. I have no access to the radio.

What is your feeling about the ICC?

I feel the ICC is not good because it may discourage other children to come back. So the war will continue.

Did you hear about the ICC while at the GUSCO centre?

Yes, someone at the centre told us that Kony was being taken to court because he wanted to overthrow the government.

Do you think the commanders will be angered by the work of the ICC?

I think so, because they will feel deceived about the amnesty. But I think Kony won't understand the magnitude of the atrocities he has committed.

Concerns about the court

A local council officer at Lalogi IDP camp made this comment in the course of a group discussion.

The ICC should come after the war ends, if not then there will be trouble for people in the community. Let's assume the rebels are still in the bush and arrest warrants are issued. No, this cannot happen; it will then mean that the rebels who are still in the bush will continue to fight until they are killed. Innocent civilians will also suffer the consequences.

Will the rebels seek revenge?

Such cases are common. Once you say anything against them they will follow you. They move unnoticed among the people. So they may kill you and all your family.

Here are some responses from people interviewed at Awere IDP camp.

[A man speaking] The issue of the ICC is not good; it will cause persecution upon the innocent civilians by the rebels and Kony himself. In Acholi, it is difficult to separate a father from his children since it breeds more conflict ... Children will assume their head/leader has been taken to court, so they will just decide to continue with the war. Therefore amnesty should be extended ...

[A woman speaking] Our greatest fear is that when he is arrested and prosecuted, his former fighters like Brigadier Kenneth Banya [who has accepted amnesty] and others might feel they are next. This might lead to another rebellion and more suffering in our land ... Maybe if they can arrest and detain him in a restricted area like Alice Lakwena, but not kill him. Otherwise his other associates, who might not have been arrested by that time, may seek revenge on the local community.

[A man speaking] What we need at the moment is this war to end, that is why we opt for amnesty. And if Kony is arrested, he should be detained in a restricted area where he is able to talk to people freely. Just like Alice Lakwena's father was arrested. Another thing is that when Kony is arrested and brought before the commission, he might include the names of those who do not deserve to be punished. This might jeopardize the peace process in the region.

[A woman speaking] Kony himself might claim he does not know what took him to the bush, he may even give false information about his collaborators ... Such an act may result in social conflicts and a tendency of revenge. Therefore he should be taken and detained in a restricted area, but allowed to meet his relatives and friends.

[An Acholi UPDF soldier speaking] According to me, there should first be agreed peace talks between the governments and LRA. When it fails, then I think the ICC can come in to prosecute them. Kony should be arrested first and taken to court. But if they issue an arrest warrant before Kony is captured then it is useless to have the court. We will just have to fight until we kill Kony.

IDP camps were also visited in Lira district – i.e. outside the Acholi area. Serious attacks here had occurred relatively recently and the living conditions were very poor. Few people had heard anything about the ICC, so questions had to be prefaced with explanations. These are some of the things people said.

[To a local council officer] *Have you ever heard about ICC?*
No, only the ceasefire. I feel this ceasefire should be there, so that the children in the bush are not killed. And about the ICC, the rebels should not be taken to court. If they are taken to court it should be after the war. If they issue arrest warrants while they are still in the bush, the rebels will be discouraged to come back. They will take revenge and kill us in the camp here ... The

107

soldiers are trying to protect us, but if you move a distance away you get them [the LRA]. It makes it difficult to get food.

[From an interview with an UPDF soldier] What I see is that the ICC should first wait for us the soldiers to do our work, and capture Kony. Later he can be taken to court for the atrocities ... When the arrest warrant is issued, there should be tight security and protection of civilians; if not the rebels will kill all of them ... The rebels might slaughter the children who are in the bush, because the top commanders already know they will be taken to court. So I say the arrest warrant should first wait ... we the soldiers have not captured Kony because he stays in a neighbouring country. But Sudan has now given us the chance. We are going to get him.

[One of the bloc leaders at Ogur IDP camp speaking] The top commanders should be taken to court because there are many atrocities they have committed on our people.

But if the ICC issue an arrest warrant to Kony while he is still in the bush what would be the implication for people in the camp?

Oh! I thought Kony would first be captured and taken to court. If it is like this [i.e. the warrants are issued while he is still free], then rebels will take revenge on us by killing us.

Lastly, here are some remarks from male former combatants at the World Vision reception centre in Gulu town. All three are young men who were abducted in the 1990s, when they were children.

(1) *Did you hear anything about the ICC while in the bush and what do you think about it?*

No, I have just heard about the ICC over the radio recently. And in my own opinion, I think the issues about the ICC might just worsen the situation at the moment because in fear of persecution the returnees might begin fleeing away and possibly back to the rebels.

(2) *While in the bush, did you hear about the ICC?*

Yes, I heard about it in the bush and often tried to discuss about it. Some of my friends would argue that if the ICC was in place then the amnesty was useless and would say all of us will be prosecuted. They argued that it was useless to come back home and be killed painfully ... So I was scared when I heard about the ICC. But I started thinking it over and said, 'After all, I am not even a commander so I may not be affected' ... When I came here I found some of my friends and they have now been discharged back to their homes. This has helped to build confidence in me. I feel a little nervous walking on the street alone thinking I could be kidnapped, but we only move in the company of [World Vision] staff.

(3) *Do you think those in the bush know about the ICC?*

Yes, I think so, especially the commanders who have access to the radios.

What do you think about the ICC?

I think the idea about prosecution is not good ... Amnesty should be extended to all to avoid further bloodshed. Otherwise it will be difficult for the war to come to an end, because Kony will continue fighting in fear of prosecution. He will not opt for peace talks. This implies more suffering for the Acholis.

An important additional aspect of the concern that the ICC will exacerbate the violence is the fear that it will endanger certain vulnerable groups, notably witnesses and children. Both these groups are explicitly mentioned in the SCiU statement of February 2004. Witness protection is certainly an issue, and it is not yet clear what the ICC will do about it.

When the ICC was described to them, many informants were

wary about the possibility of being called. According to one woman at Awere displacement camp:

> The issue of being a witness or saying something about Kony is very dangerous to us, the civilians. If you say something the next day you plus your family would just be destroyed. It has been happening in the past. For example, while you are interviewing us now, somebody might just come and hear what we say, or an LRA coordinator might even be among us. He or she will be listening to what I am saying. Later people will just realize that I have disappeared. So it is really difficult for us to comment about the LRA. I think those who will testify to the court will have to be given protection and who they are will have to be kept as a secret ... If you were to be a witness and testify, would they take you and your family away from the camp to be given protection? If not, at least Kony should be captured first ... We still fear the rebels because they come secretly and operate.

Some people I spoke to, including those who had been interviewed by the ICC investigators (see below), were clearly worried about the implications, and very concerned that I did not make an electronic recording of what they said to me. They explained that they were afraid it would appear on the radio, and then everyone would know who and where they were. There is also the issue of witnesses who have politically sensitive things to say about the UPDF and the Ugandan government – something that will become an acute problem if UPDF officers themselves end up being prosecuted. When I spoke about this to a group of senior army officers in Gulu town, they made it plain that witnesses against the UPDF would not 'be welcome' in Uganda.

Article 68 of the Rome Statute deals with the protection of the witnesses and their participation in the proceedings. Various options are possible, including 'the presentation of evidence by electronic or other special means'. It is repeatedly stressed, however, that measures adopted 'shall not be prejudicial to or inconsistent with the rights of the accused and a fair and impartial trial'. Also, Clause 5 states that 'Where the disclosure of evidence or information pursuant to this Statute may lead to the grave endangerment of the security of a witness or his or her family, the Prosecutor may, for the purposes of any proceedings conducted prior to the commencement of the trial, withhold such evidence or information and instead submit a summary thereof ... '[12]

As so often with these kinds of things, the devil is in the detail. The key phrase is 'any proceedings conducted prior to the commencement of the trial'. The implication is that at the trial itself a summary will not be sufficient. At no point is it stated that anonymity will be facilitated, nor does there seem to be provision for the allocation of new identities – although that might be a possibility. Measures were taken to allow for anonymity at the Yugoslav Tribunal, but proved to be very controversial. It was argued that they were inconsistent with the rights of the accused. So the wording of Article 68 is significant, and may limit the amount of protection to witnesses that the ICC can offer.

It should be stressed that staff at the ICC are well aware of the dangers. They recognize that security has paramount importance in dealing with any potential witness at all stages of the proceedings, including during the investigation. Informants are given the choice of ending an interview at any time and a careful risk assessment is made in each instance. It is intended to create a protective bubble around those who testify at The Hague. But there are obviously serious risks involved, as I found out myself in Gulu during November 2004. Office of the Prosecutor investigators had used their access to the relevant government minister to help obtain interviews with certain informants at one of the reception centres. I was told who had been questioned and talked to them soon afterwards. One in particular was very upset by the experience, although it was not clear if this was because of the

ICC interview as such, or because she found telling her story of abuse so disturbing. I raised concerns about these procedures in a letter to the ICC. Understandably the Office of the Prosecutor does not comment on specific investigative activities, and staff have not officially confirmed than any of the interviews took place. Nevertheless, it would be fair to say that the issue has raised worries about breaches of confidentiality. The ICC, however, has certain other options. By no means all the evidence presented in court has to be in the form of witness statements. The ICC is also bound by the Rome Statute to act in the interest of victims. That is likely to mean that many possible witnesses will never be called, and the specific counts in warrants will be affected by how evidence might be presented without endangering particular individuals and their families.

The other vulnerable group that has been highlighted is children. The danger of them being targeted and killed if the war escalates has already been noted. As pointed out in Chapter 3, however, the role of children has in some important respects been exaggerated. This is not a conflict that is being predominantly waged by children. The ICC itself overestimates the involvement of children in its 'Background information on the situation in Uganda'.[13]

> The LRA base of combatants is drawn largely from abducted villagers, particularly children, mostly aged between 11 and 15, though children younger have been taken. According to reports over 85% of the LRA's forces are made up of children, used as soldiers, porters, labourers and sexual slaves in the case of girls … The total number of abducted children is reported to be over 20,000 …

There is no doubt that children have been abducted and have been abused, but these figures cannot be correct. As we have seen, UNICEF monitoring suggests that two-thirds of those abducted between 1990 and 2001 were over eighteen, and the vast majority of those abducted were released within a year. The best current estimate is that there are about a thousand abducted children who have not returned. Most of the children from northern Uganda who are suffering are not with the LRA, but are living in appalling circumstances in the IDP camps. The LRA can be expected to continue using tactics aimed at terrorizing them, and it would be relatively easy for them to do so, even if the recent Iron Fist offensive has depleted their ranks. Such tactics do not require large numbers of combatants – just a few who are willing to perpetrate acts that are shocking enough. The emphasis on the LRA's child soldiers can therefore at times seem disproportionate.

It is a point that was not lost on some of our informants in November 2004. Here are some observations from one of them (she spoke in English):

I felt a victim of the war while I was at college, I was among the people who were abducted but it was quite lucky for me that I managed to escape. Our first-born was abducted too. She stayed with the LRA for two months ... To the women and children the war has offered them opportunities ... One of the girls [who had been abducted] told me that in the community other people said: 'I wish my daughter was also abducted. I wish my son was also abducted. He or she would be getting help from the money and would bring money for me also at home.' So people look into it as maybe the war makes other people rich, or gives them an opportunity that they did not really expect they would have. Others coming back from the captivity, they were taken for studies, they offered funding for studies until they reach university. So to other families, they look at it as an opportunity.

Emphasis on child soldiers also has other effects. It allows for the demonizing of the LRA, and deflects attention from the undeniable fact that President Museveni's government has recruited child soldiers too, and not only in northern Uganda.[14] At the same time, it allocates juvenile status to the LRA. It suggests that the rebels should not be thought of as normal adults. They are either children or they are young adults who have not matured properly, because they were traumatized and abused when they were children. There may be a degree of truth in this, but it means that when people with the LRA are killed, they are called rebels in government reports, but when they surrender or are captured they are often treated like innocent children, even if they were abducted as adults, have been military commanders or have given birth to several children themselves.

Several of those returned abductees that we spoke to at reception centres complained that their adult needs, responsibilities and commitments were not being recognized. In a somewhat similar way, the LRA commanders in the bush seem to want negotiations leading to a settlement rather than to accept the amnesty and ask, like recalcitrant children, to be forgiven. Clearly the spiritual aspects of the LRA make it hard for outsiders to make sense of their behaviour. Nevertheless, they have at times put forward a political agenda (which has incidentally included an independent judiciary).[15] They have wanted to be taken seriously. A corollary of this, of course, is that they can (and should) be held to account for their actions.

Assessment of the evidence: is the ICC exacerbating the violence and endangering vulnerable groups? With respect to the impact of the ICC on the protection of witnesses and children, there remain several unknowns. The ICC itself does not know exactly how it will deal with the former, nor has it yet made public who is going to be prosecuted or where (for an ICC response to these points, following the unsealing of warrants in October 2005, see Postcript). As far as children are concerned, we do not know whether many are in captivity, or, for that matter, what has actually happened to most of those that have returned. Partly for logistical and security reasons, monitoring has been inadequate. The numbers still with the LRA are not as high as is persistently asserted, but there is also little doubt that those remaining in the bush will be in acute danger if anti-insurgency measures are stepped up, particularly if helicopter gunships are used. This is a concern; however, it is relatively less significant than the vulnerability of children in the displacement camps. There are hundreds of thousands of these and, as we have seen, the mortality rate in some camps is already alarmingly high. They will be in grave danger if the war escalates. So, will this happen?

The LRA seems to have been weakened by the more recent UPDF (and SPLA) offensives, but it still has a capacity to resist the UPDF and potentially to perpetrate massacres. According to UN security sources, in mid-2005, there were around 300–400 LRA guerrillas based in Kitgum and Pader districts, and perhaps around twenty in Gulu district. In Sudan there seem to be 500–600 based in the area between Torit and Juba, where they have been attacking villages. There still seems to be some support coming from the Sudan army, but probably from breakaway factions that do not support the current peace process. At the end of July, John Garang, the SPLA leader and recently appointed Sudanese vice-president, was killed in a helicopter borrowed from President Museveni. This is expected to exacerbate tensions, and might mean that the LRA becomes more active. The LRA leaders have also been aware that the ICC has intervened. According to one of the recent arrivals at the World Vision reception centre in Gulu in November 2004, Kony had told his followers that there were twelve judges in Gulu already waiting to put them on trial.

The serious concerns expressed by informants and activists can therefore not be dismissed. As one of the Catholic fathers at Opit Mission put it to me in November 2004, however, 'Kony wants to talk. Maybe he fears the court.' Father Carlos himself, who has spoken out against the ICC on several occasions, now accepts that there has been less violence in northern Uganda since the formal ICC investigation started.

Here is an extract from an interview with Father Carlos in Gulu on 6 November 2004:

> When the announcement about the ICC was made in January this year [i.e. 2004], my first reaction was that the LRA have perpetrated terrible crimes, but that they are part of the conflict. We should investigate the whole conflict. Not just the last two years. It would be better to have a truth and reconciliation commission like South Africa. The whole aspect should be investigated. We need a full investigation of everything. I am not putting the UPDF at the same level as the LRA, but the government are part of the conflict. The government should have asked people, those who are the victims, if the ICC suited them. Also, there are negotiations going on with the LRA. How can those continue if the LRA are going to be prosecuted? But things have changed. Something has happened since April that we did not expect. Between April and September five hundred or so combatants have come out of the bush with their guns, including senior officers. So the ICC might not be so discouraging as we thought. Also, those who have come out of the bush have told us that the Sudan government has not been giving them anything since January this year. So the ICC may have had an influence on Sudan. The LRA will only reduce violence out of pressure, and Sudan has changed its attitude because of the ICC. They are concerned about being prosecuted. [16] It gives a powerful signal. In the past, the LRA have only wanted peace talks when they are losing. They have withdrawn when they have got new supplies and weapons. Now that Sudan is not involved, it forces the LRA to talk about peace.

The court's investigation during 2004 seemed to concentrate minds. The threat of prosecution by the ICC was probably a factor in encouraging some of the LRA to enter peace talks with a degree of urgency. When I interviewed the LRA negotiator, 'Brigadier' Sam Kolo, after his rescue by the UPDF in February 2005, he told me that he had specifically raised the issue of the ICC with Bigombe when he met her in the bush.[17] Doubtless there were also other reasons for relative improvements in security. But it is reasonable to conclude that the growing international scrutiny of what had been happening in northern Uganda was partly to do with the ICC's involvement. Various powerful countries had become more actively engaged. A British army officer was accompanying Betty Bigombe in her meetings with the rebels. The USA too had suddenly become an eager funder of the peace process, as well as supporting the military activities of the UPDF north of the border. Since Kolo left the LRA and accepted the amnesty, the peace talks have lost momentum, but there have been no large-scale massacres. Things may change, of course, when or if warrants are issued, but overall the ICC's intervention must be viewed as having had positive effects, some of them unforeseen a year ago.

The ICC is spoiling the peace process

Several activists and analysts have vehemently expressed the argument that the ICC intervention will spoil the peace process. This, of course, assumes that a genuine peace process, or a range of peace processes, is under way, and could result in a permanent solution. There are three aspects to the argument, relating to the amnesty, to the ceasefire and to local conceptions of justice. The first two have already been discussed in some detail in Chapter 4 and will be taken together here. The third requires more explanation and is addressed in Chapter 6.

It is obvious that the ICC intervention cannot be reconciled with the existing Amnesty Act, which offers a blanket amnesty to all rebels. The court was set up 'to put an end to impunity

19 Much of the discussion about peace in northern Uganda stresses forgiveness and reconciliation: posters warning about landmines and promoting 'solidarity' (Tim Allen)

for the perpetrators' of 'the most serious crimes of concern to the international community as a whole' and, as a result, it has an institutional antipathy to amnesties.[18] Under the ICC, it is no defence to claim that an accused person is covered by any kind of statute of limitations or other national laws preventing prosecution (such as presidential or parliamentary impunity). The position of the Office of the Prosecutor is that domestic amnesties are strictly a matter for the national authorities and do not prevent the exercise of the ICC's jurisdiction. In practice this means that Uganda cannot maintain a blanket amnesty if it is to adhere to the Rome Statute, which it is obliged to do. The act will need either to be formally amended or allowed to lapse. The former has not yet happened. The latter is looking ever more likely, although it may be replaced with something more reconcilable with the ICC's mandate and also more acceptable to President Museveni

– who has always been sceptical about the usefulness of a blanket amnesty. There are models that might be drawn upon to allow a partial amnesty to coexist in law with the issuing of warrants for those alleged to bear the greatest responsibility for crimes. Such a procedure could be difficult to implement, however. Several LRA commanders were themselves abducted, some of them when they were children. It will be hard to draw a precise line between those most responsible and those marginally less so, and impossible to avoid complaints about victimization.

Recognizing these problems, supporters of the amnesty have responded to the ICC with understandable alarm. The July 2004 'position paper' of Makerere University's Refugee Law Project ends with a blunt recommendation to the government of Uganda: 'Do not amend the Amnesty Act.' The following passage explains why.

> It is possible that many LRA fighters will be reluctant to surrender under the Amnesty Law for fear that they might be handed over to the ICC. The implication for those who have already surrendered is even more uncertain. While critics of the Amnesty Act argue that the limited number of amnesty applicants is an indication of its ineffectiveness, the majority of those interviewed during our research in northern Uganda see amnesty as the most feasible option to ending the conflict and ensuring that their abducted children can be persuaded to come home. Our study also demonstrated that the overwhelming majority of people believe the amnesty law is the best way to resolve the conflict. In particular, amnesty is seen as being compatible with the people's existing traditional system of justice and dispute resolution mechanisms.[19]

At the time, there was little immediate prospect of the other peaceful option of resolving conflict through peaceful negotiations. The 'position paper', however, suggested that efforts in this direction were also potentially undermined by the ICC's announcement of formal investigations. It would make it impossible to create the necessary context of trust, and any overtures would be seen by the rebels as a ploy to arrest them. As we have seen, Father Carlos of ARLPI expressed a similar view. Nevertheless, to most people's surprise Betty Bigombe did manage to broker a limited ceasefire in November 2004. When interviewed at the time, she was reluctant to discuss the ICC in any detail, but expressed reservations about its role. For Bigombe, some sort of arrangement along the lines of previous agreements with other rebel groups remains a viable option, and she has been repeatedly prepared to risk her life to achieve it. She is confident that Sam Kolo (the LRA commander with whom she has most contact) will not be prosecuted by the ICC,[20] but the threat of prosecution is certainly a constraint in discussions with others, notably Vincent Otti and Joseph Kony himself.

During research in November 2004 I found many people expressing this view. Here is an interesting exchange with Brigadier Kenneth Banya, one of the most senior LRA commanders to have been given amnesty.

What are your thoughts about the ICC – are you afraid of being charged?

I'm not afraid of being charged. I came at a time when they said amnesty. I think the government cannot make the mistake of reversing what they already have told the world. So I am not afraid of the ICC. Even though I know I was on the wrong side, I know that I never did it physically with my own hands [i.e. atrocities]. I was forced to do most of the things. But I think it is premature for the ICC to come in, as the war is not yet over. The prime ... reason ... the top commanders are not coming out has been the fear to be prosecuted. And if the ICC starts involving [acting] right now that means the war will continue. Then the war will not stop now ...

But the ICC is an international court and they decide whom they want to charge, not the Ugandan government. How do you feel about that?

.... I would say then that they have breached the sovereignty of the Ugandan government, because Uganda is a sovereign country and has its own laws. If the Ugandan government have decided to give us amnesty, then the ICC should not overlook their decision.[21]

At the displacement camp at Awere I spoke to Ojolokome Martyn, who was one of the elders accompanying Betty Bigombe in the 1994 peace talks. His views about the ICC were similar to hers: 'I think everyone in this part of the country has witnessed what Kony has done in our land. But I would rather have Kony forgiven than spark another war.'

Here is a range of other statements about the amnesty from the displacement camps – first, some typical examples of positive statements.

Amnesty is good idea, because it encourages the rebels and children to come back.

Amnesty seems very good when we look at the rate at which the rebels are returning. Those who come back speak about amnesty [on the radio]. Those in the bush are encouraged. If the government can accept it, the deadline should not be there.

Have you heard about the ICC?

No, it's our first time to hear about it. In my view, amnesty should be extended to the top commanders of the LRA.

From one of the same camps, here are less positive views:

Do you think amnesty should go on being extended?

[A woman speaking] It should just be extended for a small period.

[A man speaking] Amnesty has been given to rebels for quite a long time and maybe it is the thing encouraging them. My request is that an international body comes and helps our situation ... I support the ICC. Kony and his commanders have been granted amnesty and it has been announced over the radio. But they have failed to come back. So the court should be there.

[An Acholi UPDF soldier speaking] The rebels should be taken to court. People have suffered. The government has been calling for peace talks but they have failed many times. So it is useless to have peace talks again.

[Another UPDF soldier] Amnesty now should only be extended to those abducted and forced to become soldiers – even though they have committed a lot of atrocities. But the top commanders like Kony, Otti, etc. should face the court.

Next, here is a group of former LRA combatants, reflecting on their experiences of accepting the amnesty.

(1) *Did you hear anything about the Amnesty while in the bush?*

We heard that there was amnesty but we were told that some of us who were already fighters would not have amnesty but instead be killed. This gave us a lot of fear and I believe there are still many in the bush with such a mentality ... When I reached here, the treatment was the complete opposite from what we had heard. I learned that we were being deceived about the whole thing. The UPDF, whom we considered the number one enemy, were the ones who picked me from the battlefield and brought me here.

(2) *While in captivity, did you ever hear about amnesty?*

Yes, I heard about it but others wouldn't have had the chance to hear or talk about it. I had a friend who was already a commander and had a radio. So I would move to his home and listen to the programme *Dwog cen paco* [Come Back Home] – a programme on amnesty on Radio Mega FM. In the LRA, only those from lieutenant upwards listen to the radio freely.

(3) *While with the LRA, did you hear about amnesty?*

Yes, I heard about it once in a while and at times when I had the chance to come and loot radios among other items, I would listen to the radio before the commanders took it away ...

When you came back, were you surprised?

Yes, I was very surprised, because the commanders told us that if we came back the soldiers would detain us in a fenced place, and we would not be allowed to move freely. But when I came, there was nothing of the sort.

Do you still have friends in the bush?

Yes, I have many of them still in the bush. I think amnesty should be extended to give them time. There is propaganda among the LRA that once you report, your voice is recorded and played over Radio Mega but you are killed. So it's difficult to be quickly convinced about amnesty.

Assessment of the evidence: is the ICC spoiling the peace process? There can be no doubt that the ICC intervention is both a threat to the Amnesty Act and a limitation on peace negotiations. According to one informant involved in the latter, ICC representatives have recognized that they are 'spoilers' in these respects, and this is probably one reason why the court has adopted such a low profile. Back in January 2004, the ICC press statement on the referral recognized that 'Many of the members of the LRA are themselves victims, having been abducted and brutalised by the LRA leadership. The reintegration of these individuals into Ugandan society is key to the future stability of Northern Uganda. This will require the concerted support of the international community – Uganda and the Court cannot do this alone.'

It seems likely that ICC staff have been trying to adopt sensitive and appropriate strategies to allow positive developments to take their course, and this was confirmed in various discussions with staff of the Office of the Prosecutor both in The Hague and in Uganda during 2005. It should be added that the various communications that have been going on between the ICC and other actors involved in northern Uganda are something of a departure from previous models of international criminal prosecution. Although the Office of the Prosecutor does not comment on investigations, there does appear to have been quite a bit of listening going on, and this has been incorporated into ICC procedures. When I visited The Hague offices of the court in January 2005, I was impressed by the time and effort allocated to understanding what I and others had to say, and where possible responding to issues we raised. Such an approach is in marked contrast with, for example, the SCSL. As was mentioned in Chapter 1, in June 2003 Charles Taylor was indicted, stalling the peace negotiations that were happening in Ghana and prompting Taylor's immediate return to Liberia. Whatever the legal justification, the decision provoked a storm of controversy and prompted some African governments to refuse to serve the warrant.[22] Doubtless the ICC is eager to avoid such an incident.

With respect to the amnesty, I have not found evidence that the ICC intervention has actually undermined the process. Not enough people know about the capacities of the court for it to have made much difference. Some worries were voiced by former combatants, but if anything the ICC intervention has persuaded people to accept the amnesty in the expectation of avoiding prosecution. Moreover, local views about the amnesty are more mixed than many activists have suggested, and it has not proved to be a viable solution to the conflict, although it may still have a role to play.

Relatively few of those I spoke to in November 2004 and March 2005 told me that they thought that the amnesty was a failure or inappropriate, but this was partly because of the use of the same term in Lwo for 'amnesty' and 'forgiveness', a point discussed in the next chapter. Many informants began by stating that the amnesty or 'forgiveness' was a good thing, but would then contradict themselves by expressing enthusiasm for the prosecution and punishment of the LRA's senior commanders (as well as certain UPDF officers). Interestingly, a questionnaire-based study of 2,585 adults carried out in April and May found that this paradoxical attitude is prevalent.[23] Sixty-five per cent of respondents said that they supported the amnesty process, but 76 per cent of them also said that those responsible for abuses (including those in the UPDF) should be held to account, and only 4 per cent said that amnesty should be granted unconditionally.[24]

There have, in addition, been problems with the administration of the amnesty. Since the period in mid-2004 when many of those returning from the LRA went through the formal amnesty process, the Amnesty Commission has not issued many amnesty certificates. Several of those I have spoken to who went through the formal procedures complain that it was a waste of time, because they were not given anything to assist their reintegration. There has also been confusion about what the amnesty really means. Most of those who have passed through the reception centres for formally abducted people seem to think they have been given 'amnesty', even though they have no formal certificate. This muddle may have begun to change, because the World Bank has provided funds for the provision of mattresses, blankets, seeds and other commodities to those who have registered. But it has placed a strain on the capacities of the commission, which has a national mandate and limited resources. In August 2005, staff at the Amnesty Commission office in Gulu town were unable to provide information on exactly how many former LRA combatants and abductees were eligible for the formal amnesty, or how many had so far been given certificates.

There is a further problem too with the amnesty process which needs to be highlighted. Ideas promoted by various actors about Acholi 'forgiveness' skate over the resentment that many people feel about former combatants seeming to be rewarded for their actions. This was highlighted by the opening ceremony for the new World Bank programme on 27 May 2005 in Gulu town. It was a bizarre affair. The newly appointed Acholi Paramount Chief oversaw the proceedings. The most prominent among those being given their items were former LRA 'Brigadiers' Kolo and Banya and 'Colonel' Kamdulu. In front of a large audience they were each given their amnesty package as a kind of present to welcome them back. Kolo even made a speech about the real meaning of forgiveness. The event was photographed for Human Rights Focus, a Gulu-based human rights organization that has fiercely supported both the amnesty and traditional justice procedures.[25] The pictures were published in the organization's magazine. One of them shows Betty Bigombe handing a mattress to Banya, a man who is well known to have taken many girls as 'wives' while still with the LRA, and who has sought to gain access to some of them following his return. One wonders what use he will make of his gift! Whatever the occasion's merits as a way of encouraging others to accept the amnesty, this was hardly a good advert for Ugandan (or 'Acholi') justice. It is the kind of thing that, for at least some of my informants in northern Uganda, brings the amnesty into disrepute.

With respect to the ceasefires and peace talks, there is a general awareness that these have happened before and eventually failed. So again there is local scepticism about them. There is, in addition, a widespread view that Kony himself does not want to be forgiven by the current Ugandan government, and would not accept the amnesty even if he trusted President Museveni to adhere to it. To the extent that he and his senior commanders want an end to the war, they appear to want a negotiated settlement – probably one that allows them to live a relatively comfortable life somewhere else. This was confirmed by Sam Kolo in an interview in August 2005. He complained to me that the circumstances of his evacuation by the UPDF had meant that he had been unable to negotiate adequate material arrangements for his livelihood. An agreement with Kony and Otti will probably involve an attractive package, including provision of economic benefits and legal impunity. If so, it will obviously be in direct conflict with the ICC process. For her part, Bigombe has repeatedly stated that if warrants are issued, she will withdraw from the peace talks (although when the warrants were unsealed in October 2005, she was persuaded not to do so – see Postscript).

6 | Justice and healing

This chapter returns to a theme introduced at the end of Chapter 1. Will international criminal justice, expressed through trials at The Hague, be any more than an inappropriate imposition? Can such proceedings heal psychological wounds, establish individual responsibility over the collective assignation of guilt, and dissipate the call for revenge? Do they enable victims to be reconciled with their erstwhile tormentors; or do they violate and undermine local forms of social healing and reconciliation? Should 'the decision to seek justice through punishment or forgo punishment in favour of justice through reconciliation' be made by the victims and not some foreign authority?[1] The same kinds of question have been asked in each situation in which the new international criminal justice mechanisms have been introduced since the mid-1990s. They have been the subject of passionate and acrimonious debate, and nowhere more so than in northern Uganda.

In Uganda, there are specific reasons why the ICC has been open and vulnerable to local criticism and pressure. First, the court made an error of judgement in January 2004 when the chief prosecutor held a joint press briefing with President Museveni. From that time onwards, his office has had to struggle to demonstrate that it is not simply 'in the pocket' of the Ugandan government. Second, differences between the ICC and the other international tribunals and courts place it in a different position to both government and civil society. On the one hand, 'complementarity of jurisdiction' requires the court to make more efforts to adapt to national priorities and processes. On the other hand, Article 53 of the statute indicates that prosecution can be stopped if it is 'not in the interests of justice taking into account all the circumstances', among which is mentioned 'the interests of victims'. This suggests a requirement to take on board considerations that move beyond narrowly defined legal rules to some engagement with notions of 'natural justice'. At the very least it implies that the views of victims can affect what it is appropriate for the court to do. Significantly, an ICC paper on policy issues published in September 2003 notes, 'The Prosecutor will encourage States and civil society to take ownership of the Court ... ', and his office ' ... will take into consideration the need to respect the diversity of legal systems, traditions and cultures'.[2]

These factors have meant that the ICC has had to engage with the view that the Acholi people have their own alternative approach to justice. Certain non-governmental groups and eloquent activists have propounded 'Acholi justice' as an established truth, with some of those based in Gulu town being especially vociferous about it. They have been influential in acting as advocates for the Acholi people to journalists and other outsiders, including some researchers and expatriates working for aid agencies, and their ideas have additionally influenced local government policy, the promotion of the Amnesty Act and the presentation of the peace talks. In Gulu town, in particular, it is presented as a kind of 'received wisdom' that the Acholi people have a special capacity to forgive, and that local understandings of justice are based upon reintegration of offending people into society. In late 2004 I found that it was a perspective that had become so institutionalized that it was expressed as a matter of course at virtually every public meeting on the conflict. It also appears in most reports and articles. For example, one generally excellent study comments that the Amnesty Act

> ... is seen to be compatible with Acholi dispute resolution mechanisms: 'Culturally, people's ideas of forgiveness are

entrenched. They don't kill people; they believe the bitterness
of revenge does not solve the problem. So it was easy for people
to accept the idea of amnesty. The culture is for compensation.'
As a religious leader said, ' ... Some people say you can't give in
to Kony. But when you look at the Acholi people, they believe in
mato oput, which is a reconciliation ceremony here. In Acholi
culture there is no death sentence, because they know that the
death sentence increases violence. They practise that in their
culture, so why not in this?' Thus, there is a clear feeling that the
amnesty is based on values that are seen as compatible with the
context in which it is being applied.[3]

Not surprisingly, this contrast between international and local
approaches has been seized upon by romantically inclined pro-
ponents of 'transitional justice' and writers in search of a good
story. The *New York Times* rarely publishes articles on Uganda,
but in April 2005 chose to run a substantial piece on the topic.[4]
Here is an extract:

> The International Criminal Court at The Hague represents one
> way of holding those who commit atrocities responsible for their
> crimes. The raw eggs, twigs and livestock that the Acholi people
> of northern Uganda use in their traditional reconciliation cere-
> monies represent another. The two very different systems – one
> based on Western notions of justice, the other on a deep African
> tradition of forgiveness – are clashing in their response to one of
> this continent's most bizarre and brutal guerrilla wars ... 'When
> we talk of arrest warrants it sounds so simple,' said David Onen
> Acana II, the chief of the Acholi ... who travelled to The Hague
> recently to make his objections known. 'But an arrest warrant
> doesn't mean the war will end.' ... The other day, an assembly of
> Acholi chiefs put the notion of forgiveness into action. As they
> looked on, 28 young men and women who had recently defected
> from the rebels lined up according to rank on a hilltop overlook-

ing this war-scarred regional capital, with a one-legged lieutenant colonel in the lead and some adolescent privates bringing up the rear. They had killed and maimed together. They had raped and pillaged. One after the other, they stuck their bare right feet in a freshly cracked egg, with the lieutenant colonel, who lost his right leg to a bomb, inserting his right crutch in the egg instead. The egg symbolizes innocent life, according to local custom, and by dabbing themselves in it the killers are restoring themselves to the way they used to be. Next, the former fighters brushed against the branch of a pobo tree, which symbolically cleansed them. By stepping over a pole, they were welcomed back into the community by Mr Acana [i.e. the Paramount Chief] and the other chiefs. 'I ask for your forgiveness,' said Charles Otim, 34, the rebel lieutenant colonel, who had been abducted by the rebels himself, at the age of 16, early in the war. 'We have wronged you.'

There are several serious problems with these kinds of argument. One is that ideas about 'amnesty', 'forgiveness', 'reconciliation', and the setting aside of punitive judgment are not conceptually distinct in the Lwo language. *Timo-kica* means 'doing forgiving/ reconciliation etc.' and can be used for all of them. So talk of 'forgiveness' may not mean quite what it suggests in English. Among other things, it makes it hard to explain to Lwo-speakers why the amnesty expires on a particular date and may need to be extended. I have also found that attitudes to forgiveness or amnesty are not as consistent as is so often asserted.[5] Many of those I have spoken to begin by saying that they want *timo-kica* but go on to express enthusiasm for prosecution and punishment. Claims about Acholi forgiveness need to be closely interrogated, and certainly not taken at face value. Furthermore, there are problems with equating rituals of social healing with 'justice', as well as questions to ask about who has the right and authority to speak for the Acholi people as a whole and claim that they do not want or that they reject the ICC.

Institutionalization of 'mato oput'

At the local level, arguments against the ICC intervention have been propounded most forcefully by certain traditional and religious leaders. The lobbying has been associated with very committed and charismatic individuals who are connected with organizations such as the Council of Elders Peace Committee, the Council of Chiefs and the Acholi Religious Leaders Peace Initiative (ARLPI). It has been concentrated in Gulu, where most international agencies and journalists are based. ARLPI was established in 1998 to coordinate peace-building initiatives of the Catholic and Protestant churches and Muslim associations. In practice, the Catholic and Anglican clergy dominate it. The ARLPI and the Acholi traditional leaders' associations were both partly a product of funding from international aid agencies, and many of their public statements are jointly agreed.[6] The current consensus about customary Acholi conceptions of justice has largely emerged from the aid-funded collaboration between these groups.

In 1997, the first of several conferences known as *Kacoke Madit* (Big Meetings) was held in London. The idea was to create a forum for all Acholi people working for a peaceful resolution of the conflict in northern Uganda. Following the 1997 conference, research was commissioned on the views of Acholi 'opinion leaders' in Uganda about peace and reconciliation. An influential report called *The Bending of the Spears* was subsequently written by Dennis Pain.[7] The author is both a passionate enthusiast of Acholi culture and a charismatic Christian.[8] He argued that the armed conflict was eroding 'Acholi culture' and that what was needed was a community-based approach drawing on Acholi values and institutions.

A particular ceremony known as *mato oput* (bitter root or juice) was highlighted. Mediated by elders, it requires the wrongdoer to admit responsibility, ask for forgiveness and agree to pay compensation. Both parties drink the blood of sacrificed sheep mixed with *mato oput*, and the ceremony ends with *gomo tong* (the bending of spears) to represent reconciliation. In fact the report mixes up two separate ceremonies here. *Mato oput* is a ritual performed to reconcile social divisions after a case of killing. It deals with the consequences of homicide. Those who play the main part in performing it are the wrongdoer and a representative of the family he or she has harmed (and clan elders). *Gomo tong* is performed to seal the resolution of conflicts between clans (or perhaps other kinds of groups). It is a ceremony of peacemaking. The last time it was performed may have been in the early 1980s, as part of the efforts made to reconcile divisions between the people of Acholi and the people of West Nile following the fall of Amin. It was also famously once used to celebrate reconciliation between the Payira and Koch clans. A conclusion of Pain's report was that a blanket amnesty was needed, but would not be sufficient. It was also necessary to have the support of Acholi chiefs so that *mato oput* and *gomo tong* could be conducted, something that would require funds for compensation.

In 1999, finance was offered by the Belgian government to undertake research on Acholi chiefs and build on Pain's findings. The work was carried out under the auspices of ACORD, an NGO that had been working from Gulu town for a long time. Working with government officials, local councils and religious leaders, researchers made efforts to identify 'traditional chiefs' – known as *rwodi* in the plural and *rwot* in the singular. In 2000, Acholi 'traditional chiefs' were formally (re)instated, and the Rwot of Payira in Gulu district was elected to become the Acholi Paramount Chief. Efforts have subsequently been made to perform collective '*mato oput*' ceremonies. Initially they were performed in the main towns, but they are increasingly being conducted in IDP camps too.

In November 2004, the Acholi Paramount Chief Elect, Rwot

133

Onen David Acana II, was reported in the government's *New Vision* newspaper as opposing the prosecution of Kony and other rebel commanders, and asserting that:

> The best way to resolve the 18-year old-war in our region is through *poro lok ki mato oput* [peace talks and reconciliation] as it's in the Acholi culture ... I wonder who will help them in giving evidence to prosecute Kony since the Acholi do not buy their idea of taking him to court because the Acholi have forgiven all LRA rebels and their leader Kony of crimes committed against them.[9]

The odd translation of *mato oput* as 'reconciliation' here is important. Through the process of re-creating or reinvigorating the system of *rwodi*, the term *mato oput* has been allocated a more generalized, or rather a different, meaning. Other old rituals, notably *nyono tong gweno* ('stepping on eggs'), are also sometimes referred to as '*mato oput*' in this context. The term has become a sort of euphemism for healing rites or blessings performed by the *rwodi moo* (anointed chiefs), which promote reintegration of former LRA combatants into society by offering 'forgiveness'.[10] In an interview (in English) a few days after the above report was published, Rwot Acana reiterated and elaborated his views.

> We the traditional leaders do not want to be seen to be blocking justice. We emphasize our justice system of reconciliation. I told the ICC prosecutor when I met him in London that the timing is not right. Religious leaders are negotiating. Also we have a letter from rebel commanders saying that they want to talk ... It is a fluid situation. Confrontation is still going on ... The LRA are in the bush. The Sudan government has not signed the Rome Treaty. So how will they get the LRA? Military means have been going on for years. It has not worked. The ICC does not have an army ... It is like a hostage situation. Someone is holding a child from a high building and says I will jump with the child. Then

you come with flags and a warrant. It will not help. The LRA is suicidal and reacting to the situation. They want people to think they are powerful. The LRA will act so that lots of lives will be lost. What will the ICC do if they massacre people again? It will add to the crying ... Also the senior commanders of the LRA were probably abducted themselves. We failed to stop them being taken and being turned into what they are today ... We have the blanket amnesty. And we have the traditional culture. When someone kills we have a system to stop the killing. That is why we did not have death as a punishment. Nor did we have jail sentences. Rather we had reconciliation – *mato oput* ... Does the ICC not value community values of people? Does the ICC override all other systems? Even if Kony is taken to The Hague, that will not be a punishment. The prisons there are air-conditioned! Rather he should be in the community. He should see the suffering he has caused. Here people look in your eyes and say I forgive you. Then he will understand and recognize what he has done ...

Christian religious leaders also discuss the concept of *mato oput*, although in a slightly different way. By and large the Protestant clergy seem to be more willing to become involved in supporting this 'pagan' ceremony than Catholics, but the difference is slight. Both Christian groups locate traditional Acholi rituals within their agenda of promoting or creating a truly Christian society, drawing on ideas of sacrifice and purification (or even sanctification) through the acceptance of suffering.

The following is from an interview (in English) with one of the Italian Catholic priests at Opit Mission.

In the villages the people welcome them back [those abducted by the LRA]. A girl recently came back after six years – with children from the rebels. Her father was there to welcome her. People were clapping and welcoming them. They know that she and the other children were forced to go with the LRA ... I have not noticed myself any trouble with the returned people integrating ... We talk about reconciliation. They feel forgiveness. Rituals are all right for pagans, but they are superficial. But for someone with faith, they receive the sacrament. I don't discuss pagan rituals like *mato oput* with them. For a Christian, it is Christ. They are saved in the sacrifice of Christ ... Some have been shocked by what they have done or seen. They come for confession, and they feel relief that it is secret. Acholi beliefs are based on fear. *Mato oput* is right, but it is God who puts that forgiveness in their heart.

The retired Anglican bishop of Gulu, Bishop Baker Ochola, is one of the ICC's fiercest local critics. Here he explains how his antipathy is linked to both his Acholi identity and his Christian faith.

The children are the victims. Bringing in the ICC at this stage is bad. The government is part of the conflict as well. The ICC is wrong ... Those who have come back, if they are prosecuted, what kind of justice is that? ... The government says it has killed so many – are they rebels or abducted children? If they just investigate the LRA it will be an injustice to society. It will destroy peace efforts and the amnesty law. The amnesty has done a lot to make the children come back. Even the top leadership, they should also be forgiven for the sake of peace. Impunity is not understood in world understanding of justice. God brings mercy. Even in our culture. The mercy of God allows us to deal with impunity. We don't say revenge should not happen. Justice means that you know the truth, and then arrive at peace. For the children who have suffered at the hands of the LRA and UPDF, there is no better justice than to end the war ... In Western society how you look at life forms your values. So if someone is found guilty they are punished. But that is not healing. Justice is to stop people committing crimes with impunity because they do not know God. God has revealed *mato oput* to our society – to taste the pain in our society, to taste pain and suffering and death ... Both sides take the root. Anyone who comes from outside must maintain impartiality ... You must go back many years. You must dig deep. Law is not made in the way we look at it. Law is holy. You can learn about justice. We say that where the LRA have abducted our children, killing them will not solve our problem. What we can do is to show them that we are different to them. Acholi know that it is only through forgiveness that the problems can be solved ... The good of society is to forgive. That will help society coexist ... Reconciliation is the only way. The truth will be known and responsibility accepted. They [the ICC] will do what they want, but they will never have the consent of the people to do that ... We are against injustice. It is not in our nature to be unjust.

Individuals such as Bishop Ochola, it needs to be stressed, are regarded with considerable respect, not least because they have sometimes acted with remarkable courage – liaising with the rebels, standing up to the government and assisting the afflicted. The Catholic Church in particular has enormous prestige, having kept the mission hospitals running throughout the troubles. So it is not surprising that the views of these traditional and religious leaders are accorded weight and significance. Their promotion of forgiveness played a significant role in pressurizing the Ugandan government to pass and, more importantly, to be willing to implement the Amnesty Act, and they have also been very successful in furthering the idea of forgiveness through various NGOs and the local council system.

Several local NGOs and local council officers are in fact closely associated with the traditional and religious leaders, and are openly enthusiastic about their conceptions of peacemaking. A meeting was convened for me to discuss the ICC intervention with the Gulu District Reconciliation and Peace Team in November 2005. Of the ten activists who attended, seven turned out to be representatives of the District Local Council (LC5), and all began by expressing the same opinions as Rwot Acana and Bishop Ochola. International aid agencies too have tended to accept traditional and religious leaders' insights as accurate reflections of local beliefs and practices. Moreover, arguments about forgiveness are reinforced by the (mis)perception of the war as one that is being largely waged by children on children. By definition, this makes the perpetrators of atrocities less responsible for their actions, and has meant that aid agencies and local councils have been concerned about the protection of those accepting the amnesty. For example, by-laws have been passed making it an offence to disturb people who have been with the LRA once they return home, and these have been interpreted to mean that it is unacceptable, or at least inappropriate, to argue that forgiveness should be limited or denied. People seem to be embarrassed or ashamed of wanting accountability and revenge. Generally it is not something that they say in public meetings. In private, however, things are different.

I shall return to the co-opting and expansion of the concept of *mato oput* later in the chapter. Before doing so, here are selections of extracts from interviews. They offer a rather different set of views about forgiveness and criminal prosecution than the 'received wisdom' allows.

A diversity of local views

Particularly in Gulu district, it is unusual for people to admit in a public venue that they wanted revenge or recompense, although there was a willingness to talk about prosecuting Kony and the senior commanders, and there were differences of opinion about whether or not this was a good idea. Generally informants were willing only to talk about their personal desire for punishment and retribution in private. Here is a typical exchange with a group of local council officials; it took place at Awere IDP camp.

Have you heard about the ICC?

No, it's our first time to hear about it.

What are your views?

Well, amnesty should be extended to the top commanders.

How about the ICC?

The issue of the ICC is not good; it will cause persecution upon the innocent civilians by the rebels and Kony himself. In Acholi, it is difficult to separate a father from his children since it breeds more conflict. Children will assume their head/leader has been taken to court, so they will just decide to continue with the war. Therefore amnesty should be extended.

Did you have many returnees from your area?

Yes, many are coming back; brigadiers, captains and other low-ranking officers.

How does the community receive them?

The community does receive them well because we, the local councils, sensitize them not to take revenge or harm the returnees. If you had the time you would talk to them so that they can assure you they are really free.

Is there no problem welcoming the rebels back?

No, there is no problem.

Even for mothers who have lost their children?

We really try to tell the mothers to try and forget all about what happened in the past and continue with normal life for peace to prevail.

How can a mother forget her child killed innocently?

Yes, they cannot forget but we try to tell them not to discuss issues that will force those who were affected to seek revenge.

In complete contrast are the views of Walter Ochora, the chair of the Gulu District Council – one of the few Acholi living in Gulu who has been willing to stand up in public and call for prosecution and punishment. He is an interesting character with a colourful past. He had been a senior army officer in the UNLA and had played a significant role in the coup of 1985, which brought Tito Okello to power for a short period. After the NRA seized Kampala, he fought in the UPDA, but was one of those who accepted peace terms. He has known Kony for a long time, and has had contact with the LRA, notably in June 2001 when he initiated a peace dialogue in a temporary 'demilitarized' zone. I was introduced to him in a bar in Gulu town as someone looking into the risks of the ICC intervention. He immediately assumed I was likely to be opposed to it, and asserted that 'Kony is a criminal', and that he should be prosecuted and sent to prison. At a discussion meeting on the ICC hosted by Save the Children in Gulu in August 2004 he was one of the only participants to be unequivocally supportive of the ICC's role. Here is what he said (he spoke in English).

When it comes to the business of the ICC I am very grateful for the performance of this court worldwide. If you have been following international relations it is actually demystifying the issue of international leaders being above the law. We hope that the court will bring a bit of sanity to the world. Normally in society there are norms and laws. That is why there are always sanctions to make sure that these norms are followed. They are divided into two. If you do well you are given a reward and if you do the contrary you are punished. For example, in the army – the army is licensed to kill, at the same time if you murder you go for court martial. There is a difference between killing your enemy and murdering your enemy. We have the Geneva Conventions. You cannot capture the enemy and then murder them. Those are the laws that govern men.

There has been a lot of confusion about the way the Acholi have their norms and sanctions. The *matu oput* is there. What

I know about *matu oput* is that you first have to admit that you have committed a crime and that you are repentant. Then the process goes from there. When you look at the LRA you see that there are those that have committed atrocities. There are those who see that they have committed crimes against their own people and these are the ones that are coming out in big numbers. The amnesty has been there for years but they are only responding now. I have been in touch with the LRA for a long time both when I was brigade commander and in civil society ... Some told me a few days ago that even if there are only five left they will still continue. For various reasons they get promoted for crimes. To them they take their ranks very seriously. They have a reason to stay in the ranks. They have free women. There are many reasons for those guys to stay in the bush ...

Kony made it very clear that as long as he is still active he will remain in the bush and those that have left the bush he would destroy. How do we stop this? I am someone who is really pro the move by the prosecutor. The ICC will not stop the LRA coming out. I want to allay the fear that the ICC will stop them coming. Those boys who are ready to come will come and those who are not ready will remain. But we need to set a precedent that those who commit crimes unabated should not be able to get away with it. The ordinary citizens have not given their comment on the ICC. It is always coming from the top leadership ... We should move to our community ourselves and talk to them about this thing.

My experience of doing what Walter Ochora suggested – talking to people out in the IDP camps – has been that his views are shared more widely than has been supposed. It would seem that a consensus has been established that needs to be interrogated and deconstructed. Things are by no means as straightforward as they have been made to appear. Here are a series of interview extracts taken from less public environments (they all took place in the Lwo language). The first took place after a meeting with the Gombola chief (i.e. the government-appointed chief – a civil servant) and his staff at Anaka. From his facial expression, it was clear that one person at that meeting thought that things were being said that were just for public consumption. I took him aside and asked him what he thought.

> *What do you think about the ICC?*
>> It should put pressure on people in the bush.
>> *Should the ICC prosecute all of them?*
>> The top commanders should be the ones prosecuted. We need to say that terrorism is wrong. If those commanders took your kids and forced them to do things, would you say you would not fight them?
>> *Some people say even the top commanders should be forgiven.*
>> But I don't want to forgive them. We have to make them know it is wrong. We don't want to forgive. My brother was killed by Kony. And my sister. He tried to abduct them. They escaped, so he killed them.
>> *What about rebels who have returned home? What do you think about them?*
>> Some are in the community here. We just allow them back. It is by force. People say there is a local law. You are not allowed to say that is the one who killed my sister. No one may point a finger and accuse. But in the mind it is there.

The next extract is also from a 'chairman' of a local council (LC3) at another displacement camp. She is a woman, and spoke very frankly:

> According to me the people are very open to the ICC because Kony has committed atrocities. He has refused to come back home when people have tried to talk to him. Some people say they should kill such people. Some want to forgive them. Most people think they should go to court ... When people keep

extending the amnesty, people just go on killing. The ICC makes them think they will go to court if they don't stop ...

What do you think when someone who has killed comes back here to live?

It is not good. Those people made a lot of atrocities here. People do not see them in a good way. Those people should be sent somewhere else, and kept there for a long time. Forgiveness is not possible in the local community. God forgives them. But people do not think like that.

To give an example of what she means, here is an extract from an interview with a man living in the same camp. He refers to Sam Kolo, who subsequently accepted the amnesty.

Those people [the LRA officers] fear to come back. They don't fear the government. They fear the civilians. For example, Vincent Otti. He fears to come back because he killed hundreds of people in Atiak. He fears the civilians. Other commanders killed in Lira district. Sam Kolo killed in Alero. He made many atrocities. They now fear to come back. It is the young commanders who have done the really bad things. They cannot come back. They fear what the civilians will do.

What about the women – do people forgive them, those that have come back home?

The women go looking for husbands here at home [i.e. they look for men to live with]. Their activities are dangerous. They fight with men, and when they fight it is a war. People fear them. They cannot remarry after being in the bush. They join the UPDF or the LDU [Local Defence Unit].

Do people fear them because of cen (polluting spirits)?

Yes. People fear them because they are polluting. They will not greet you by shaking hands. They are not friendly with us and do not trust us. In the bush they covered themselves in oil. If people have not been anointed like that, they do not greet them [i.e. they greet only those who have been 'purified' by LRA rituals]. If they do greet you, it is only out of fear. Some were living with the LRA for ten years or more. They have that wild mentality.

This extract is from an interview with a woman at another camp. Her son had been abducted by the LRA a few months before.

Do you forgive them for taking your son?

No, I will not forgive them. They picked my son. They do not show forgiveness to me, why should I forgive them?

If he survives, if he comes back, will you forgive then?

No, I will not forgive them.

Have you heard about the ICC?

Yes, I heard about it on the radio.

What do you think about it?

They should prosecute. But the commanders will go wild if there is a warrant. So if they cannot be arrested quickly, just kill them. Don't take them to court if it takes time. If you take him [Kony] to Europe, that will be no good. He will escape.

The following is from an interview with another woman at a nearby home. She was in her forties and was sitting in her tiny compound, surrounded by graves with rocky surfaces, indicating violent deaths.

Yes, they should take the top commanders to court. They made lots of atrocities. Have you seen the graves? They are my relatives and children – even a schoolboy. He went to collect food. They killed him.

Do you look at returned rebels and say to yourself, 'Is this the one that killed my child?'

We see them – but we do not see them badly.

Why not?

Even if we see them with bad eyes it is useless now. If you see them you must just forgive. Maybe it could be your son who was taken. What to do?

(At this point a drunken man at the edge of the compound starts to sing a Protestant hymn, one sung at burials. Someone comments: 'We drink so much to forget our problems.' I move to the side with the woman I was talking to, because she seems to want to tell me something.)

How do you feel about forgiving?

I do not speak about it. If I talk I will lose all my people. I just want them to come home. I can't say any more ... (*she starts to cry*).

Most at the camp, one of the worst affected by LRA attacks, were enthusiastic about the ICC, once its role was explained to them. Here are comments from two elderly men, interviewed separately.

(1) *What are your views about the amnesty and ceasefire?*

If the peace talks and amnesty are there, people should come home.

What about prosecution for the commanders by the ICC?

The commanders should go to court. Let them be charged.

(2) *Should Kony come back home?*

No, they should arrest him and take him to court. All the commanders should go to the court.

The chair of the local council at the camp also had very clear views about prosecution, and expressed them incisively in fluent English. In addition he made some interesting observations about the ideas about healing promoted by the traditional leaders in Gulu town.

Have you heard about the ICC?

It's a bit late. We give the go-ahead. We heard about international bodies in other places but not here. The amnesty has done a lot – although the army claims that it is they who have really done it [by forcing LRA soldiers to surrender]. Now the LRA is like a wounded buffalo. When they hear about the ICC ... when they hear that they will be prosecuted, they will use guns. The ICC has to be quick, with international warrants of arrest for the biggest commanders ... I do not forgive Kony or Otti [a senior LRA commander] – why should they kill people? Me personally, I don't forgive. These Acholi are killing their own people. There are also notorious commanders on the government side. They also committed inhumane acts ...

How do people react to returned rebels?

It depends. The majority are OK, and some are productive. But there are those who have psychological torment. They are not staying well with people. Some are also over-drinking ...

Do you perform rituals for them?

Yes, we have prayers, and also various things to help heal them. The *rwot* [traditional chief] is involved in it, and the elders. However, they cannot reach the proper *abila* [ancestral shrine], so they do it here.

What about the ceremonies performed in Gulu by the new Paramount Chief?

The *rwot* here is negative about that. So am I. Each clan must do their own healing. It is a wasted effort to put resources with the Paramount Chief at Gulu.

Lastly, here is a rather revealing exchange about *mato oput* with a man in his thirties living at the same IDP camp. He has been abducted by the LRA three times. Twice he was released after a few hours and once he managed to escape during an ambush by government forces. It would seem that he does not so much want to forgive as to forget.

If you met one of those who abducted you after they came back, what would you do?

I would not fight them.

146

Why? When someone kills your relative, do you forgive them (i.e. timo-kica)?

Yes, we do. There is one here who killed his brother-in-law.

Do you talk to him?

Yes. We even drink beer with him.

Do people say anything about what he did?

No.

Has he performed mato oput?

No! He would fear to do that.

Why?

To do that he would have to say I am the one that has done a bad thing. He would have to ask to be forgiven by the family he had killed from. That will be difficult. How could you live with a person who said that they had done such a thing? So we just look at him like a normal person [i.e. we ignore what has happened] ...

In saying that 'we just look at him as a normal person' the meaning seemed to be 'we pretend that we do not know what he had done'. In my interviews in late 2004 and early 2005 I found many people shared this kind of view. Also, the idea that some kind of external agency might intervene to allocate accountability and punish those found guilty seemed more appealing than activists in Gulu suggested. When I circulated the findings for discussion in northern Uganda in February 2005, they not surprisingly proved controversial with certain local activists. The results of the recent questionnaire-based survey carried out by the International Center for Transitional Justice and Human Rights Center, University of California, Berkeley, suggest, however, that they may be representative of widespread attitudes.[11] Of the 2,585 adults interviewed in April and May 2005, 66 per cent wanted punishment for the LRA and only 22 per cent favoured forgiveness or reconciliation. Of those respondents who had heard of the ICC, 91 per cent thought it would contribute to peace and

89 per cent thought it would contribute to justice. It was striking also that only around 10 per cent of respondents looked to 'Acholi traditional and religious leaders' to represent them or to bring justice or peace to the region. Enthusiasm for such figures was highest in Gulu district, but even here, only 15 per cent thought that 'traditional leaders' best represented them, and only 6 per cent thought that 'traditional leaders' could bring justice. On the other hand, many respondents were positive about 'traditional ceremonies' as a way of dealing with the LRA. Around 50 per cent of respondents in Kitgum district, 60 per cent in Gulu district and 70 per cent in Lira district gave responses indicating that they thought they would be useful. An implication seems to be that rituals are very important, but 'traditional and religious leaders' much less so. The following sections help explain why.

Chiefs, churches and spirits

Members of staff at ACORD raised concerns about the policy of externally supporting 'traditional chiefs' as part of the peace process right at the start. A few months into the research programme that was being funded by the Belgian government to build on the findings of Dennis Pain's *The Bending of the Spears*, they noted that healing and cleansing rituals were occurring, but that reconciliation rituals were much weaker. In addition, they pointed out that young people were less desocialized than *The Bending of the Spears* had suggested, but they no longer automatically respected elders. Questions were raised about the emphasis in Pain's work on the views of 'acknowledged "opinion leaders"', rather than ordinary people, and it was observed that the research had created tensions between some elders, as there were expectations about financial benefits.[12] It might have been added that much of the work of collecting information about *rwodi* had been done before by, among others, J. P. Crazzolara in the 1930s and 1940s and J. B. Webster and his colleagues at the History of Uganda Project in the 1960s and early 1970s. Moreover, the traditional roles of *rwodi* and clan elders had already been much analysed and debated in the published literature.[13] Indeed, anyone acquainted with the existing literature on the Acholi might have predicted that there were going to be significant problems with the approach being taken.

On 17 January 2005, Rwot Acana II of Payira was crowned Paramount Chief of the Acholi. President Museveni attended the coronation and the *New Vision* newspaper claimed that he was the '24th hereditary leader in a dynasty that began in 1420 with Rwot Luo in Shiluk Bar-el-Gahazel, Sudan'.[14] This has required a great deal of myth-making, including the remarkable early date,[15] and for many Acholi people the setting up of a paramount chief is actually a violation of traditional customs. In the past there was no such thing as a paramount chief, and the numerous *rwodi* had a collaborative relationship with the elders of each clan associated with them. Many were essentially rain-makers and arbitrators rather than having political power, although some had adopted certain chiefly rituals from the kingdom of Bunyoro. Several were appointed administrative chiefs by the early British administration because they needed local authority figures to implement indirect colonial rule. During the early years of the protectorate the most influential of these included those who had forged alliances with the nineteenth-century ivory traders and invaders from Egypt, obtained guns from them and acted as local war leaders and agents. These included Rwot Olia at Atiak, Rwot Ogwok of Padibe and Rwot Awich of Payira.

The earliest accounts of chiefs in the region come from the journals of the Victorian explorer and adventurer, Samuel Baker. In the book about his first expedition in the early 1860s, he noted that there were no 'big chiefs' in 'Shooa' country, but during his later expedition in the 1870s he met Rwot Ocamo (Baker calls him Rwotcamo), the chief of 'Payira', who claimed to be the ruler of the whole of 'Shooli'. Later writers demonstrated that this could not have been the case, or at least that 'Shooli' did not include other parts of what become known as Acholiland in the early twentieth century. Rwot Ocamo was actually at war with other clans and chiefdoms in the region, and the Rwot of Payira seems to have been affiliated as a kind of vassal to the kingdom of Bunyoro. In the 1870s, however, Ocamo had obtained guns and support from slave and ivory traders and seemed to be trying to assert a degree of independence and authority. He collaborated with Baker, who was at that time a mercenary in the employment of the Khedive of Egypt and launching brutal raids against those who would not accept his (and theoretically the Khedive's) authority. After Baker's departure, Ocamo continued to wage wars against his neighbours, but he seems to have had conflicts with some of the Nubi soldiers that Baker had left behind. The Rwot of Padibe managed to obtain their assistance, and was able to defeat Ocamo in 1877. His head was cut off and placed inside his own 'royal' drum, which the Padibe warriors had captured.

Ocamo's successor, Awich, continued to fight his neighbours in the same way, and was apparently successful in capturing cattle and girls in great numbers, although he did not manage to recapture his father's head. He managed to recover it only in 1923 as part of the bridewealth and dowry exchanges that occurred when one of his daughters married Rwot Olia of Atiak.[16] In the 1880s and 1990s, with support from Bunyoro and some of the remaining Nubi soldiers, Awich managed to assert a degree of control over territory running from Kitgum to Pakwach. During that period he had accumulated an estimated 400 to 500 guns. To put this in perspective and to give an idea of the scale of the armed raiding, in 1913 the British administration collected a total of 5,000 guns from what became Acholi district.

Awich's power waned dramatically at the end of the 1890s when his enemy, Rwot Ogwok of Padibe, formed an alliance with the British officers sent to the area. Awich was captured and imprisoned at Nimule in 1900, being replaced as Rwot of Payira by his brother. He was reinstated by the British administration two years later, and then made a very interesting and important decision; he sent an invitation to Protestant missionaries in Bunyoro. He did not convert to Christianity himself for another forty years, but he shrewdly realized that he could play one group of Europeans off against another. It was the beginning of a strong relationship between Payira and the Christian missions, one that has recently celebrated its hundredth year. After an uprising in Lamogi in 1912, the British deposed Awich again and deported him to Kampala. He returned to his home area in 1920, partly at the instigation of Rwot Olia of Atiak, but was not reinstated as *rwot*. An assessment of his life written just before his death in 1946 by a sympathetic colonial officer declared him to have been a failure.[17] He was certainly less successful in political terms than Ogwok or several other Acholi chiefs. Nevertheless, his invitation in 1904 helped establish Gulu and Kitgum towns as important centres for the Catholic and Anglican churches, and his imprisonment under the British protectorate has lent him and the chiefdom of Payira a certain status.

Under protectorate rule there were several attempts to place the Acholi under a paramount chief. It was thought that this would make indirect administration more efficient. The model used was based on the administrative arrangements made with the kingdoms of southern Uganda.[18] All these attempts were resisted, however, because of differences of opinion about who should take on such a role. Also, the initial policy of appointing government chiefs from the established *kal* (chiefly) lineages changed. Government chiefs began to be appointed as straightforward civil servants, and were expected to have educational qualifications. These chiefs came to be known as *jagi* (singular *jago*) or sometimes 'gombola chiefs'. This undermined the political influence of many *rwodi*, although they usually continued to be accorded considerable respect within their clan, and in some cases also by affiliated groups of *lobong* ('commoner') clans. They also continued to participate in important collective rituals, notably those connected with rain-making and dispute settlement between clans.

The old tensions between the most important *kal* lineages, as well as tensions that opened up in the later protectorate period between *kal* clans and other clans, have not disappeared. There does now seem to be a general willingness to have a Paramount Chief, but there is a widespread view in some quarters (especially in Kitgum district) that the elders of Payira have used their links with politicians, NGOs and religious leaders to inappropriately assert themselves. Moreover, the current Rwot of Payira, Onen Acana II, is an educated young man. While he is widely viewed as a very decent, intelligent and likeable person, for some of my traditionally minded informants he is too much under the control of the established Christian churches, and does not really understand or share 'real' Acholi customs and traditional beliefs. At the same time many younger people find the efforts to create new chiefly rituals around him rather ridiculous. Caught between competing demands to be traditional and modern, he has an uphill task to establish credibility outside his immediate circle of supporters.

The attitude of the Catholic and Protestant clergy towards traditional beliefs is complicated. There is a willingness to incorporate or reinterpret some local customs from a Christian point of view, particularly when they support the idea of forgiveness. Historically both churches have preached against 'Satanic' practices and initially put a great deal of emphasis on converting *rwodi*, such as Awich. Ancestor veneration was discouraged, and chiefs and elders were told not to perform healing ceremonies at ancestral shrines (*abila*). There was, however, a more lenient attitude towards *ajwaki* (i.e. spirit mediums, witch doctors and healers). This was partly because they were initially viewed as relatively insignificant. They were not perceived as 'traditional leaders' and many were female. Also, as we have seen, many asserted a strong Christian faith, and some would even refer to themselves as *nebi* (Christian prophets or teachers). In addition, the status of Acholi possession cults was confused from the late 1940s by the spread of the Balokole movement from other parts of East Africa. The Balokole were fundamentalist Protestant revivalists, who criticized the lifestyles of the established clergy. They, too, preached against 'Satanism', but embraced Pentacostalism, exorcism of 'demons' and the laying on of hands. Given the ambiguities in the Lwo language with respect to *tipu maleng* (pure spirit/s) and the third person of the Trinity, the connections between Christianity and local possession beliefs were reinforced. They became even more important for local diviners in the years immediately after independence, when numerous 'witches' were rounded up by order of chiefs. Many of those accused were tortured and some killed. Diviners or 'witch doctors' had to be careful to assert their moral probity by linking their activities to Christianity (or, in some cases, to Islam).[19] Such associations have remained important. In the mid-1980s, both Alice Auma 'Lakwena' and Joseph Kony were *ajwaki* and both had a relationship with the Catholic Church that was at least tolerated.

For obvious reasons, in recent years the established churches have tended to preach against *ajwaki* (and *nebi*). The Holy Spirit Movement and the LRA have also sometimes killed them as part of their campaigns against 'witchcraft' and competing interpreters of the spirit world. As a result *ajwaki* have become secretive. Whereas in the early 1980s it was common to hear the drums of a seance, these are now rarely heard. I have found that local council officers tend to deny that there were any *ajwaki* in their displacement camps. Others explain that they have introduced

153

local laws to control them, because there is a concern that the activities of *ajwaki* will attract the LRA and lead to attacks. It is, however, easy enough to locate *ajwaki* by talking to people individually or in their own compounds. Those *ajwaki* I have spoken to say that they have to operate quietly and they have introduced different ways of divining that do not involve drums. They also explain that *cen* (polluting spirits) could not be treated with such methods. If exorcism was necessary, they took their patients and their patients' families out into the bush to do it. But it was a dangerous thing to do, both because of the LRA and UPDF soldiers, and because the *cen* themselves could be very powerful.

Here are some extracts from interviews to illustrate these points. First, some comments from the old man who is acting as the Rwot of Atiak. This interview took place in November 2004 (in Lwo). It should be added that when I spoke to him again in March 2005 he was much more enthusiastic about Rwot Acana. He had thoroughly enjoyed the coronation in Gulu town. Nevertheless, he reiterated the point about clan elders performing *mato oput*.

How do you feel about the appointment of a paramount chief?

That is just temporary. If there is going to be a paramount chief, the Rwot of Atiak must be the Rwot of Acholi. Even the British sent robes to my predecessor, Olia. It was Olia who went to release Awic [the Rwot of Payira] when he was taken to jail … This new thing is politics. It all started when Philip Adonga of Padibe was made overall chief in 1958. But that was just for administration.

Can the Rwot of Payira perform mato oput *and other healing ceremonies?*

No, that has to be done by the elders of each clan [*kaka*]. This thing they have been conducting in Gulu is not good. But what can I do? They accepted to do it there. They must do it separately. If they do it in the town it will make things worse. It will bring *cen* there ...

Esther Aluk is an elder from Kitgum. She is well known as someone who has accumulated a great deal of knowledge about Acholi customs. She was involved in discussions with Dennis Pain when he was preparing his *The Bending of the Spears* report in 1997, but she is appalled by the current developments. She spoke with great feeling in a mixture of Lwo and English.

It is no use performing healing rituals in town. The thing they are doing now is a big mistake. It will take all the *cen* to the place where it is done. Those rituals have to be done by clan elders. The Acholi are losing their culture. Culture was created by God. I am very Christian. Jesus goes with my culture. I love God so much. I respect Catholics. They brought Jesus to us. But they must correct their mistake. I helped set up the Acholi Traditional Ritual and Prayer Committee. We collected information and messages from old elders and summarized them. Instead of listening, the *rwodi mo* [the anointed traditional chiefs] are fighting those people. It is because the religious leaders are mobilizing the *rwodi mo*. They are saying the old ways are Satanic ... I have also been with *ajwaki* and asked them about their spirits ... Some *ajwaki* are bad, but some do not want to kill. Some just want money – they are just thieves. But some of them are real *ajwaki*. We need a meeting for *ajwaki*. I even asked the Church of Uganda to be involved. Let us talk to *ajwaki*. Let us find out how the spirit came to Kony. Some say they can destroy the spirit. The elders of all the districts should sit together. The Verona Fathers should call a meeting for *ajwaki*. They should not say not to do so. They should talk to them ... Let us be one. There should not be a paramount chief. Acholi should follow their traditional culture ... The elders of Payira just used politics to make the paramount chief thing happen. They wanted the money that aid agencies gave for it, and they joined up with the Religious Leaders Peace Initiative in Gulu. They are fighting against the real rituals. We need to mobilize the elders for prayers and rituals. I don't want *rwodi mo* interfering.

I also talked to Esther about the current peace talks, the amnesty and the ICC. She was very sceptical that any of these will help much. The key issue is to deal with Kony's powerful and evil spirit, which she claims is essentially the same as the one that had possessed Alice.

Peace talks? What about the spirit? Kony may agree to talk, but you have to find the spirit. Museveni does not have a spirit, and Kony's spirit may come shouting, 'No! no! no!' Some say that the [bad] spirit is not there with Kony at the moment. But it will come back and spoil everything. It may jump to another person. It jumped from Alice to Lokoya [i.e. her father] to Kony. It may jump again. If they arrest him, will they arrest the spirit? It will jump elsewhere ... If they arrest Kony, the spirit will just continue. It is the spirit that has forced Kony to do things. He was an *ajwaka* before the war. He was healing people. The father of Kony came to my home. Both his sons were *ajwaki* ... That was always that family's work – even the grandfather. But that [bad] spirit entered him [Kony] one day at 10 a.m. It made him climb up into a tree. The spirit spoke through him and said that he must go to fight. Even if Kony has killed my brother, I forgive him. I don't want to kill him. He did not plan it. Other old people think the same as me, but not the young ... Young people do not know about such things. They don't like to hear about it. We need to perform ceremonies to deal with the spirit. It is not just people who are crying. Spirits are crying too. We need to deal with the [bad] spirit. But young people don't want to finish things in that way. The old people who know the rituals are passing away. But if they are not performed we will all die. I don't know what will happen ...

156

Many other informants raised the issue of Kony's spirit or spirits too. Ojolokome Martyn, the elder from Awere who accompanied Betty Bigombe at the 1994 talks, observed that 'Kony is a demon-possessed man. Such people are uncommon here and they normally do things unknowingly or out of their consent. Kony acts under the influence of demons. I was actually in the team that went to meet him with Betty Bigombe. I was unable to understand what he said unless it was interpreted.'

Like Esther Aluk, one of the *ajwaki* I interviewed at Awere had known Kony before he turned to fighting. Most of the text of the interview is presented here, because it raises issues of local healing and reintegration that are simply ignored in much of the current discussion about the role of traditional leaders. Like all the other *ajwaki* I spoke to, she is a woman.

Have you been assisting people affected by afflictions and spirits?

It's true I have been helping people. The spirits that make me able to do so came in my dreams. At first I tried to resist but they began inflicting on me afflictions ... that made me faint with epilepsy. Whenever I fainted, I saw angels who urged me to take up the job of being an *ajwaka*. I tried to resist, telling them I was a Catholic since my birth ... The persistent sickness made my husband divorce me and later sent me back to our home. Unfortunately I had lost both my parents but my only brother took me back. So with all this I submitted to the spirits and they began showing me herbs to cure certain diseases and how to send away the evil spirits in children from the bush.

Where do you send those spirits?

The spirits are sent somewhere and buried.

Do you think your spirits are clean/holy?

The spirits are holy and four in number, each of them tells me their name.

How do they appear?

They appear in priestly gowns and with rosaries around their neck, holding Bibles.

What are their names?

The leader is called 'Odora' and his other name is 'Oyeyeng'. This means earthquake. The others are Labeja, Kalawinya and Abayo.

So other spirits sometimes come?

No, only the four that I mentioned. And after me accepting their work, they showed me some medicine that cures epilepsy and they told me that I would never suffer from epilepsy again.

What language do the spirits use?

The three spirits use Acholi with the exception of Abayo, who speaks British English. Kalawinya translates for him.

Are they the spirits of the dead?

Yes, they are spirits of the dead. I did not see them but I believe their spirits wander and come to me because when they are not in me, I feel normal. But if they are in me I feel something different inside me ...

When you had these spirits, did you go to see another ajwaka?

Yes, and he said that the spirits were the ones disturbing me. So I was trained from the village before coming to the camp. The spirits have now stayed in me for eight years ...

Was it not expensive to get trained?

Yes, it was, I had to spend 10,000 shillings.

What kind of people come to you? Are they also bothered by spirits or do they want to become witch doctors?

Yes, those possessed by polluting spirits (*cen*) and those who have other kinds of wild spirits (*jogi*) come to see me. Often the problem comes in the form of sickness and affects their children. After trying the hospital in vain they come to me for help ... These days it is the returnees [those who were with the LRA] who come and behave in funny ways or run mad. The four spirits always tell me what medicine to use and they are cured ...

They were mainly abducted and made to kill or passed over dead bodies [i.e. were affected by *cen*]. They might have also watched someone being killed while in captivity, sometimes from the same village. It can make them run mad.

Do you think the cen *made them run mad?*

Yes, if they are possessed, they say what they have been doing in the bush. Sometimes they carry pangas or knives to cut people.

Are those who fail to get treatment from you dangerous?

Yes, they are. If the spirits come in them, they carry axes, pangas or a hoe with an intention of cutting someone. Such acts do not happen all the time, but are seasonal [i.e. they happen sometimes] ... Before these children come home, they pass through centres [i.e. GUSCO and World Vision reception centres]. When they come home they start experiencing demons and that's when they are brought to me for treatment ...

I also asked her whether she was worried about LRA attacks on *ajwaki* and whether her activities were supported by everyone in the camp:

I am always afraid, that's why I am in the camp. But whenever Kony is coming, the spirits inform me and even tell me which direction he is coming from and where he is going... Kony is a mad man who does not give an ear to any of us *ajwaki*. He has actually killed them and even cooks them. He forces the clients he finds at an *ajwaka*'s home to eat the *ajwaka*'s body. Some people in the camp feel I am doing something bad and have a negative attitude towards me, but the work is necessary ... there are also many other *ajwaki* working here too ...

Finally, she had some very interesting observations about Kony himself.

I think the spirits are influenced by an individual's own character ... Once a spirit comes over someone it only gives the person the power to do their heart's desires. Therefore Kony had something wrong with his ancestral spirits and thus the spirits that came over him made him do the evil things. I remember Kony himself was an *ajwaka* to whom I took my son 'Ojok' for treatment of his umbilical cord – which had stayed for three months without healing. Kony referred me to his brother 'Ayeyo', who was also an *ajwaka*. Kony claimed he had to go to consult his spirits at that time. So it was his brother who helped my son. Later, before starting the atrocities on the Acholi people, Kony started by killing that very brother of his. So it depends on what kind of person you are. I once asked the spirits why Kony was behaving in such a way. They made it clear to me that Kony and his family had sacrificed a human being at their shrine at home [i.e. their *abila*]. So it's the spirits of this person seeking revenge combined with other evil spirits that are possessing him.

The evidence on healing and justice

It is entirely appropriate that priests should encourage Christians to forgive. 'Turning the other cheek' is an important aspect of the faith. It is also remarkable how some Acholi Christians seem to be able to act in this way. Similarly it is understandable that Christian leaders and traditional leaders influenced by their teaching should promote indigenous versions of Christian teachings. Even for non-believers, assertions about Acholi understandings of moral justice or Acholi notions of forgiveness are very seductive. Nevertheless, they must be treated with caution. Most of those I spoke to in the displacement camps mixed concern about the security implications of issuing warrants for the arrest of Kony and his senior commanders with a willingness to see them prosecuted and punished. Certainly there was no general rejection of international justice. Instead there was concern about how such legal measures are going to be applied, and why it has taken so long for their plight to be noticed.

20 A *mato oput* ritual performed at Pabbo IDP camp in August 2005, one of scores of such ceremonies that have been encouraged and facilitated by various agencies involved in promoting peace: representatives of the family that com-

mitted the killing and the family that lost a member jointly submit to the healing process (Ben Mergelsberg)

21 Drinking a concoction make from the blood of two slaughtered sheep mixed with *mato oput* (the 'bitter root') (Ben Mergelsberg)

22 A host of NGOs attended the ceremony, and photographed each detail. But was this really an 'authentic' healing ritual, and does it have much significance for the peace process? (Ben Mergelsberg)

To the extent that there was ever an integrated Acholi justice system, it was introduced and regulated under the indirect rule of the British protectorate. Government-appointed chiefs were empowered to hold courts, and could dispense punishments such as beatings, but they were not allowed to execute the accused. To that extent, it is true that 'traditionally' chiefs and elders did not impose the death penalty. Individuals were, however, killed when the chiefs became more independent in the 1960s, usually when they were found guilty of 'witchcraft', a term that could cover a variety of behaviours or traits. Those accused of being witches were, it seems, often marginal individuals who might also be thought to be thieves or responsible for a wide variety of misfortunes.

If 'traditional' refers to pre-colonial practices, then a great deal has to be speculative. A recent report by one of the groups that has been encouraging *mato oput* ceremonies to be performed under the auspices of the new Paramount Chief and his council of rwodi has noted that the ritual was rare in the past because, 'according to elders ... "few killings existed in pre-colonial times" due to the strong social fabric that guided Acholi behaviour'.[20] This has to be understood as myth-making. There is ample evidence from historical studies and from the early accounts of explorers that killing was very widespread indeed in this region of Africa, particularly between the later 1860s and 1910s. Moreover, the Acholi did not exist as a discrete 'tribal' group until the early protectorate. What life was like before the mid-nineteenth century is largely unknown, but the oral histories of Crazzolara, Atkinson and others do not make it sound harmonious. Doubtless systems of accountability that bound populations together were complex. All social groups have spoken and unspoken rules of behaviour and modes of social interaction. But there is no evidence that there existed some form of detailed pre-colonial 'Acholi' legal code in a modern sense. It is very likely that clans (*kaka*) had customs to control levels of violence between relatives and with allied groups. Armed conflicts would also have been resolved by negotiation on occasion. But this must be the case among just about every African population studied by anthropologists since Evans-Pritchard's classic analysis of 'segmentary opposition' among the Nuer.[21] Although they might not always be applied, knowledge of rituals of reconciliation and the payment of blood compensation is widespread. So there is nothing particularly unusual about *mato oput*. It is one of a number of terms used for different kinds of purification, social healing and dispute settlement that have been described in the region. They are an important cultural resource, but they have not stopped many individuals being killed in the past, nor have they prevented collective killing between closely related groups.

Their purpose is usually to interpret the spirit world and the experience of misfortune, and to re-establish or make manifest appropriate social relations. They are often linked to public acceptance of certain social hierarchies, including gendered hierarchies, and the making explicit of certain shared moral norms. It should be added that the ceremonies and ritual behaviours that become important at any particular time are by no means always old ones that are taken 'off the peg', but rather ideas about old models are often used to help shape new ones.[22] They are also likely to be as concerned with setting aside or 'forgetting' wrongs as recalling them and 'forgiving'.[23] More ominously, they may be harnessed for divisive or violent purposes. They may be used to promote the internal coherence of groups and the exclusion of outsiders, or they may be an aspect of witch-killing cults. It is worth remembering that both Alice and Kony have relied heavily on the adaptation of healing rituals for sustaining the loyalty of their followers. The former was able to gain the adherence of numerous former UNLA soldiers partly by performing rituals of cleansing for those that had been affected by *cen* from the killing in Luwero during the early 1980s.

163

At present there is plenty of evidence that various forms of social healing play an important role in what is happening in northern Uganda. The LRA continue to initiate their recruits with cleansing rites, including anointment with oil. In the IDP camps and towns *ajwaki* and *nebi* still practise their forms of spirit possession, divination and exorcism. Clan elders, sometimes including *rwodi*, perform rites associated with ancestor veneration. The Madi, Langi and Teso also have their own rituals, and all the groups borrow methods and healers from one another. There are, in addition, Christian rites, which some say they find more helpful. For Catholics, individual confession and collective celebration of the mass are claimed to have therapeutic effects on those who are disturbed or traumatized.

Since November 2004, my research team and I have interviewed more than two hundred individuals who have been with the LRA and have returned to live in the IDP camps or in the towns. Their experiences have been very mixed. Many have had to cope with outright hostility, even from immediate family members. Almost all state that they have been involved in some kind of healing ritual, and it is usual for them to say that it was useful. Often they claim that it made them 'lighter' or 'calmer'. Praying to God in a group is sometimes highlighted by those that have passed through the World Vision reception centre. For others, the performance of rituals by family members and elders confirmed their status as social and moral persons. Studies carried out by various agencies, including NUPI, Caritas and the NGO Forum, have similarly shown that the performance of such rites is widespread. Some researchers, however, seem to have been carried away by their enthusiasm for them, treating them as 'a kind of magic bullet to solve any kind of conflict'.[24] For example, one researcher claims that 'up to 80 percent' of those interviewed who have gone through 'cleansing' state that 'their nightmares have disappeared'.[25]

Interestingly, the foregrounding of *mato oput* in public discussion, as well as interest from researchers, seems to have made versions of the old ritual more popular. Sverker Finnstrom attended four *mato oput* ceremonies performed by elders in the course of his fieldwork in Acholi areas of northern Uganda between 1997 and 2002.[26] But they now seem to occur much more frequently. For example, one research group claims to have documented twenty-six '*mato oput*' ceremonies between 2000 and 2005 in Pajule and Lapule in Pader district alone – although it is not exactly clear what was actually done on each of these occasions (i.e. whether it was the old ceremony or some new variation of it).[27] In early August 2005 a *mato oput* was performed at Pabbo, attended by my research team as well as those of Caritas and other NGOs. I showed the video of the occasion to Tonny Odiya Labol, who had been Finnstrom's Acholi collaborator. He complained that it was not a 'real' *mato oput* at all. The elders, he claimed, did not even know how to the cut the sheep in half in the correct way.[28] For Tonny, people are just playing with customs and do not really understand them. A significant aspect of this particular ceremony was that it aimed at reconciling clans divided by a killing that occurred fifteen years ago. All the *mato oput* ceremonies documented in Pader also involved killings in the general population. I have not yet come across any confirmed instance of *mato oput* being performed to reintegrate a former LRA combatant, although this is often claimed to be taking place.[29]

The confusion seems to arise primarily from the activities of the Paramount Chief and the council of *rwodi*. They have not attempted to perform *gomo tong* ('the bending of the spears'). As far as I know, that ceremony has been performed only once in living memory, and that was more than twenty years ago. To perform it now would require the LRA to come in from the bush and participate as a group. What they have done is perform blessing ceremonies for former LRA combatants of the kind de-scribed in the *New York Times* article (quoted on pp. 130–1). These are sometimes called *mato oput* but really draw from a range of Acholi customs, especially *nyono tong gweno* ('stepping on eggs'). *Nyono tong gweno* is a ritual that just about anyone can perform, although it should be performed at someone's own home. It signifies acceptance back into the community after a period of absence, particularly when the person has done something im-moral or amoral, such as having a child while living away from the ancestral home. It has been adapted in this new context as a ceremony to 'forgive' the LRA.

Mato oput of this kind has been performed for all the senior LRA commanders who have accepted the amnesty. I spoke to 'Brigadier' Sam Kolo in March, soon after he had been rescued by the UPDF, and just before he went through the healing rite. I asked him whether he was going to perform *mato oput*. He said that he was, but I pressed him on the topic and asked whether he would really look into the faces of those he had harmed and agree to pay compensation. To this he replied that he would not. He would just do the thing that the Paramount Chief was responsible for. I asked him whether he thought the ceremony really meant anything. He smiled, indicating that he did not.

Perhaps such ceremonies play a role in promoting the Amnesty Act, but this is hardly a unique system of Acholi justice. From the evidence it is possible only to conclude that such a thing does not exist. It may well be that some processes will emerge over time that link adapted healing rites with an arrangement for dispute settlement. Perhaps the *gacaca* system introduced in Rwanda might provide a model. There are also examples closer to home. In Moyo district during the late 1980s I found that the local council system (at that time called the Resistance Council system) took on this kind of role, acting as informal courts, and drawing on local understandings of accountability and moral probity.[30] They played an important role in rebuilding social accountability among the Ugandans who had returned from refugee settlements in Sudan. But they did not always act in ways that most human rights activists would think of as 'just'. They helped reassert patrilineal authority, and sometimes accused individuals were tortured and even killed. Is this the kind of thing that activists in northern Uganda want?

From all this discussion my own position is surely clear. Rituals of healing are common, but most of them have nothing to do with the new council or *rwodi*. Nor do they confirm that accountability for crimes has been set aside by the community as a whole. I have found no widespread enthusiasm for *mato oput* or other ceremonies performed by the Paramount Chief. On the contrary, some Acholi people I have spoken to are adamant that such public rituals are useless, or make things worse by concentrating *cen* in the urban centres. Not surprisingly, Madi, Langi and Teso informants are even more dismissive. They have also suffered at the hands of the LRA, so why should it be the Acholi who do the forgiving? Moreover, the emphasis on Acholi customs as a means of dealing with the LRA has other unfortunate connotations. In Uganda, especially in the south of the country, there is a tendency to demonize the Acholi people. For political and cultural reasons they are caricatured as innately violent. It is not uncommon to hear people in Kampala say that they should just be left to get on with their war on their own. All the talk about the Acholi forgiving those among them who have killed and mutilated can seem to reinforce the perception that they are not like other people and have their own ways of managing themselves. In my experience, the majority of Acholi, Madi, Langi and Teso who have been affected by the war want a more adequate security response to the situation and some form of legal accountability for those who have abused them, both in the LRA and the UPDF. One of the questions asked in the

2005 survey of adults carried out by researchers from the International Center for Transitional Justice and the Human Rights Center, University of California, Berkeley, was 'What is Justice?' The most common responses were 'compensation': 8 per cent; 'assistance to victims': 10 per cent; 'truth and fairness': 11 per cent; 'reconciliation': 18 per cent; and 'trials': 31 per cent. Just 7 per cent of respondents mentioned 'traditional justice'.[31] People in northern Uganda require the same kinds of conventional legal mechanisms as everyone else living in modern states. Far from there being widespread antipathy for the ICC, those that know about it are generally positive, and concerns expressed about it are mostly to do with the way in which it might secure arrests.

7 | Conclusion: a learning process

At the beginning of 2005 there was some expectation that the war in northern Uganda was finally coming to an end. On 5 January Betty Bigombe said that 'The whole thing looks very promising. We are continuing to explore more contact with the LRA with a view to a peaceful settlement to this conflict. It is a question of time.'[1] A few days later, John Garang, the SPLA leader and now 'first vice-president designate' of Sudan, stated that the LRA 'are unwelcome in our territory'. Interestingly he added that they will be 'treated as enemies of the United States' – reflecting the US involvement in the Sudan peace deal, US assistance for the Iron Fist offensive and the inclusion of the LRA on the US list of terrorist organizations. The LRA seemed isolated and under acute pressure.

In March, however, the peace talks ran into problems, and the LRA showed that it had retained its cohesion and capacity to organize attacks. There have been no more large-scale massacres since May 2004, but intermittent mutilations, abductions and killing have continued. The situation in northern Uganda in mid-2005 remains tense. Pader and Kitgum districts are especially prone to attacks, and several hundred LRA combatants continue to operate on both sides of the border with Sudan. In July an unclassified document was released by the US State Department to US embassies. It noted that there are indications that some elements of the government of Sudan may be continuing to provide support for the LRA, and referred to a meeting at The Hague in April at which representatives of the USA, the UK, Norway and the Netherlands decided to develop common strategies towards ending the war. The memo proposes a tripartite arrangement between the SPLA, the government of Sudan and the government of Uganda. It ends by instructing embassies to brief 'appropriate interlocutors' on the US effort to encourage a tripartite effort against the LRA and to seek their support. An implication appears to be possible cooperation on security issues. President Museveni, however, is apparently not very enthusiastic about losing direct control of his armed forces on his territory or in Sudan. In addition, the death of John Garang, on 31 July 2005, has raised fears that the Sudan peace agreement may collapse and the LRA reassert itself.

Meanwhile, well over a million people continue to live restricted and impoverished lives in IDP camps. Many of those returning from the LRA pass through reception centres, where they undergo some basic psycho-social counselling. They are then supposed to be reunited with their families. Others return to their homes without ever formally reporting. Those who have been with the LRA for more than a short period usually go through some sort of ritual to return them to society, just as rituals had initiated them into the world of the LRA. Various healers, including female *ajwaki* and *nebi*, Christian activists and ritually significant elders and *rwodi*, have become involved in trying to contain their *cen* (polluting spirits) and wild behaviours. The local councils have also made it clear that people should not accuse such returnees of atrocities and should accept them as part of the amnesty and peace process. In many cases this has 'worked', and former abductees and combatants are living in the IDP camps or in the towns. There has, however, been very little follow-up of those who have returned, and not much is known about their day-to-day experiences. I am currently running a research project on the issue. One disturbing finding is that some of those who have come back find their current lives even worse than life 'in the bush'. They point out that when they were with the LRA they were free to move about and could obtain a variety of food, at least until Operation Iron Fist made cultivation in Sudan difficult.

Many also say that they have experienced a degree of persecution, even from within their own immediate families. They tell us that things usually started quite well, but that after a while it became apparent that they would not be receiving any more commodities from aid agencies. Then things would begin to deteriorate. Several returned women complain that their children are called bad names and are treated spitefully. These children were born while their mothers were with the LRA, and their fathers are LRA commanders and soldiers, most of whom have not accepted the amnesty and are never going to pay any bridewealth to the mothers' clans. The young children themselves often have no clear clan identity (*kaka*). Normally they would gain the *kaka* of their father, but that is not going to be possible. Where a woman returns to her father's home with a child, in theory the child will have the original *kaka* of the mother (i.e. that of her father). But many people are reluctant to accept such children born in the bush into their lineages, not least because it would give the children claims over clan lands when people are able to leave the displacement camps.

They will not be the only ones for whom claims to land may be bitterly resisted by relatives. In the future, who obtains land and by what means is going to be a major source of conflict.[2] For many people too, IDP camps are where they have always lived. Will they even want to go and live in rural places without shops, bore holes or roads? One reason why thousands of children migrate to Gulu and Kitgum at night is that there is electricity, lights and sociable company. Will they want to go and live in a village? In a baseline health survey carried out by MSF-Holland in October 2004, people were asked about their future plans. In some camps over 70 per cent of respondents said they would not go home immediately.[3] Those were new camps. In the older camps it is possible that many will feel that they are already at home and have nothing to gain from moving. A long-term effect of the war will be urbanization. Strategies need to be in place to support small-town development. Otherwise, thousands will end up in slums at the edge of the major centres.

In several instances that we came across, the local hostility to those who have returned from the LRA was intense, and people were living with the local UPDF or LDF soldiers for protection, or have been persuaded to join up themselves.[4] Others have moved to different parts of Uganda, or have taken refuge from their own relatives at the urban centres (such as the girl quoted in Chapter 3, who was forced to kill her own mother). The situation is by no means as bad as it could be. We have not come across any case in which neighbours had killed a returned rebel or one of their children. Also, staff associated with the reception centres have the impression that returned children are generally being treated better now than they were a couple of years ago. They claim that this is linked to efforts aimed at 'sensitization of the community' to the children's needs. It may be so, although monitoring is not adequate enough to make such statements with confidence. Whatever the case at present, violent incidents can be anticipated when the close regulation of life in the displacement camps ends. It cannot be assumed that local customs will allow communities to re-emerge without pain. Gendered hierarchies will be imposed, and various kinds of recompense will be sought by those who are able to demand it. Processes of social healing will be complex and sometimes brutal, as they have been in other places, including other parts of northern Uganda. This is certainly something that is feared by some returned people themselves. To give just one example, after we had interviewed a young woman who had been taken by Kony himself as one of his many 'wives', she asked us to come back and talk to her again later. When we returned, she had washed and dressed her two children and introduced them to us. 'They are the children of Kony,' she explained. 'If I take them out of the reception centre they will be killed. Where can I take them? What is the ICC going to do about it?'

For the ICC, the situation in northern Uganda has been a learning process. The complexities of the situation were seriously underestimated at the start, and it took time for the court to adapt. The Registry, the part of the court that is supposed to deal with logistics and dissemination of information, has been largely inactive, although it is currently advertising jobs in Kampala. The Office of the Prosecutor has continued to make occasional brief visits, keeping a very low profile and avoiding public confrontations with its more extreme local critics (while continuing to talk to them in private). Warrants have been prepared and could be issued at any moment. There is speculation in northern Uganda that there are already 'sealed' warrants, and their existence has not been made public (this was indeed the case – see Postscript). Perhaps this is true, but the court is biding its time. It is prepared to act swiftly when the time is right. What that means in practice is that it is waiting until it can be fairly sure that its warrants will be effectively served and that the security fall-out can be contained in such a way as not to place people in the IDP camps at risk. In other words, it is waiting until its donors decide that the peace talks and amnesty have ceased to offer any possibility of a comprehensive settlement, and are prepared to ensure that there is adequate protection for the population. The discussion about a 'tripartite' arrangement in the memo from the State Department suggests that moves are in process to make that possible. One source who has been party to the discussion has indicated to me that the use of 'special forces' might be a possibility. A crucial aspect of these developments is, of course, the new role being taken on by the USA.

The Bush administration remains hostile to the ICC, but it has become more pragmatic. A hugely important event for the court occurred in March 2005 when the USA allowed the Security Council to refer the situation in Darfur. Members of the administration had made statements about genocide occurring in this part of Sudan for some time, and had wanted an international criminal institution to investigate and prepare indictments. It was suggested that the mandate of the Hague Tribunal might be extended. The ICTR in Arusha has been very expensive, however, and the USA has been among those members of the Security Council demanding that it quickly wind up its activities. Persuading other members of the Security Council of the need for a new part of the Hague Tribunal for Darfur was not going to be tenable, unless the USA paid for it. Moreover, when the issue was examined by members of Congress they noticed that, contrary to what they had been told, the ICC prosecutor had very limited powers. Given that the ICC was up and running, and was already being funded by other donors, an ad hoc referral of Darfur to the ICC seemed to be the only sensible option. If the court can respond to Darfur in a relatively efficient way, and refrain from giving the impression that it is any kind of threat to US citizens, then further Security Council referrals may follow.

A Security Council referral potentially gives the ICC more power than a state party referral. But the court is being cautious. It has clearly learned from mistakes it made in Uganda and it is determined not to repeat them. Things have been kept at a low profile from the start. There have been no press conferences giving impressions that are difficult to reverse. Public statements have been carefully thought through. The last, released on 6 June 2005, reads a bit like a statement of what, in retrospect, was probably the sort of thing that should have been spelled out at the start of the Ugandan investigations. It says that the chief prosecutor has decided to open investigations. He has made this decision having reviewed the document archive submitted by the UN International Commission of Inquiry, and after requesting 'information from a variety of sources, leading to the collection of thousands of documents'. His office had 'interviewed over 50 independent experts'. The statement also includes a carefully worded comment from the Chief Prosecutor himself: 'The investigation will require sustained cooperation from national and international authorities. It will form part of a collective effort, complementing African Union and other initiatives to end the violence in Darfur and promote justice. Traditional African mechanisms can be an important tool to complement these efforts and achieve local reconciliation.'

It is certainly the case that, unlike in the Ugandan intervention, efforts have been made to talk to the academic specialists on the area and to find out what kinds of complexities the court is likely to confront on the ground. This time the Office of the Prosecutor is going to be well briefed. Also, the sentence about 'traditional African mechanisms' suggests an intention to head off local antipathy before it can take on a life of its own.

The references to 'complement' and 'complementing' in the Chief Prosecutor's comment are probably meant to echo the requirement of the ICC to 'complement' national courts. Whatever the specific legal connotations of the term in the Rome Statute, its use makes the court seem less threatening to entrenched interests. A further lesson learned from Uganda, however, is that 'complementarity' can produce difficulties in practice, and ones that are likely to re-emerge elsewhere. It will be interesting to see how, or if, a Security Council referral makes a difference in Sudan. In Uganda, acting in a complementary manner with national institutions has made it impossible for the court to create the impression of objectivity, and it will only be able to establish it for the people living in the war zone if it does end up prosecuting some UPDF soldiers or Ugandan government officials. Even if it does not do so, most people would still approve of the LRA being prosecuted. But it will be perceived as a kind of 'victors' justice'.

The court could in theory prosecute someone representing the government if they can be shown to be 'most responsible for the worst of crimes'. As I have explained, however, it will be impossible to do this without the government's support, and it is hard to think of an individual on the government's side for whom it would be possible to obtain a conviction. This is not to suggest that the UPDF and the Ugandan government have always acted with probity or with the best interests of the population in mind. Clearly abuses have occurred. But it would be hard to put together a strong enough case for conviction at The Hague.

Another issue that has become apparent in the course of the Ugandan intervention is the significance of repeated references in the Rome Statute to the court acting in the 'interests of justice' and in the 'interests of victims' (Articles 53, 54, 55, 61, 65, 67, 68). Taking these interests into account, Article 53 states that the Office of the Prosecutor can make a case to the Pre-Trial Chamber not to proceed with prosecution.

When I spoke to staff at the ICC in January 2005 they were confident that this would not mean that the prosecution would be delayed or stopped in the Ugandan case. By July that had changed. When I asked again about stopping the prosecution I was told that, as the chief prosecutor has recently said in public, it is possible to 'suspend' the prosecution if it is not in the interests of justice. I asked what that meant. 'Suspend' is not the same as 'stop'. The answer was not exactly clear, but implied that prosecution might be suspended if there is a comprehensive settlement, but that impunity was impossible. This is not quite what it says in Article 53. There a procedure is outlined for making a case to the Pre-Trial Chamber when the Office of the Prosecutor (OTP) concludes that there is 'not sufficient basis for a prosecution', because it is not 'in the interests of justice'. So far as I am aware there is no immediate prospect of such a case being made. Staff of the OTP have now indicated, however, that it is possible that such a case might be made at some point. It provides a 'legal' explanation for the warrants not being served – and perhaps leaves the door open for Kony to surrender in the (misguided?) expectation that he will not be arrested.

It also leaves the meaning and implication of the phrase 'in the interests of justice' and 'in the interests of victims' unresolved. As has been indicated in Chapter 6, the statute of the ICC has raised some very serious issues concerning these terms for international criminal justice. Acting 'in the interests of victims' invites the obvious question: who has the right to make that decision? In northern Uganda there are many who claim to speak for victims, but their claims are questionable. Acting 'in the interests of justice' is if anything even more problematic. It invites broad-ranging discussion of what justice means in different circumstances and in different parts of the world. It leaves the ICC open to criticism if it is seen to be adhering to a narrow, 'Western', punitive conception. But what is generally understood as criminal justice has emerged in courtrooms. What are the consequences of pushing it in a different direction? Will it not lose its already limited specificity and capacity? In setting up the ICC, there was never the intention to bring justice in a broad sense to all people. The primary purpose was to end impunity for those most responsible for the worst of crimes. It was hoped, perhaps wrongly, that convictions of evil individuals would contribute to making a better world. In northern Uganda, myth-making about local, 'restorative' justice has been taken to extremes by some activists. Does international criminal law really have to engage with this in a serious way? In doing so there is a danger of providing credibility to ideas that are closely linked to influential local interest groups. If the ICC is going to go down this path, it had better start employing some good legal anthropologists.

One way in which the ICC has tried to deal with the hostile

reaction it has confronted on the ground in northern Uganda has been to try to sideline some activists and cooperate more closely with those with whom it is possible to build up a relationship. In March 2005, the Chief Prosecutor invited a group of leaders from the Acholi community to The Hague. It was an astutely chosen group. It included Rwot Acana, the Catholic archbishop of Gulu, the Anglican bishop of Gulu, an MP from Gulu, an MP from Kitgum, and Walter Ochora, the local council chairman for Gulu (who is quoted in Chapter 6). Away from the local environment it proved relatively easy to have a more productive exchange of views. Following the meeting the Acholi delegation made a statement to the effect that it had been very successful, and that they had asked the prosecutor to address the following: (a) 'that he is mindful of our traditional justice and reconciliation process', (b) 'that he is also mindful of the peace process and dialogue, that is why he is continually assessing the situation', and (c) 'that whoever has already benefited from amnesty will not be investigated or prosecuted by the ICC'. The chief prosecutor also made a statement. He explained that he had invited the Acholi leaders to hear their views, as he had a responsibility to take into account the interests of victims and the interests of justice. He made it clear that he is mindful of traditional justice and reconciliation processes and sensitive to the leaders' efforts to promote dialogue between different actors to achieve peace. On the amnesty issue he refrained from comment, other than to reiterate that it was his clear policy to focus on those who bear the greatest responsibility for the atrocities committed.

For the court, the meeting proved to be a shrewd move. It wrong-footed academics and activists who wanted and expected the religious and traditional leaders to be unequivocally opposed to the intervention, particularly those expatriates who had adopted this position with such vigour. It also irritated representatives of other affected populations. Once again it seemed to some that

23 Protection from LRA attacks may have improved in recent years, but it is far from comprehensive. The LRA still have the capacity to launch attacks, and many government soldiers stationed out in the IDP camps are part of Local Defence Units rather than the formal UPDF. Some are very young and inexperienced (anonymous)

the Gulu elite were asserting their primacy as advocates of the suffering. But this was good for the ICC. Suddenly all sorts of local leaders and politicians wanted to hold meetings with the ICC at its headquarters. As a result, another delegation went to The Hague in April. This time there were representatives from the whole of the war-affected region. At the end of it a joint statement was issued. It made similar points to the statements at the end of the first meeting, but significantly left out reference to those who have already accepted the amnesty, and also appealed to the government of Sudan to continue cooperating with efforts to bring peace.

These meetings have inevitably been criticized in certain quarters. For those most passionate about 'forgiveness' and traditional justice mechanisms, they reflected pressures being exerted by the Ugandan government, and have served to divide the Acholi

A learning process

179

leadership.[5] But others, like the ICC itself, have been rethinking and refining their positions. Save the Children released a new statement in March, confirming its support for the work of the ICC in ending impunity and drawing attention to some of the specific concerns about the intervention I have raised in these pages.[6] In July the Refugee Law Project of Makerere University published a paper, by Lucy Hovil and Joanna R. Quinn, called 'Peace First, Justice Later', which offers a serious and very interesting discussion on the nature of justice, and suggests ways in which the 'retributive justice' of the ICC might be reconciled with a more developed form of African or Acholi 'restorative justice'.[7] In different ways, these commentators share my reservations about the risks that will arise for forcibly abducted people and the populations in the IDP camps when warrants are publicly issued. So far as it is possible for him to do so, however, the chief prosecutor has indicated that measures will have to be in place for him to be able to take that step. Any status that the ICC has accrued in the course of its short existence will quickly evaporate if things go seriously wrong. Adequate security is a prerequisite, and from the perspective of Gulu in August 2005 it is hard to see how that will be provided by the UPDF alone.

Nevertheless, I do not agree with the conclusion (and title) of the latest Refugee Law Project report that peace has to be achieved first and then justice aspired to later. Too many wars go on for too long as it is. Other strategies to resolve them have frequently been shown to fail. Has a policy of criminal investigations and prosecutions ever been tried with enough vigour to assess its efficacy? The role of the ICTY comes closest, and the evidence tends to suggest that criminal indictments can have the effect of undermining the authority of individuals and constraining their actions even when they are not yet in court.[8] Some of those promoting traditional justice in northern Uganda might respond by arguing that trials may work in Europe, but the Acholi people have different understandings of what should done to those who harm them. I am personally not convinced. My Acholi friends are like decent people everywhere else. Their way of life is special, even unique. But that does not make them 'a race apart'. Most Acholis want those responsible for terrible crimes to be held to account, and in northern Uganda, as in Europe, it is possible for trials to contribute to peace-building. 'Humanity' is not 'too thin a community upon which to base a universal right to punish'.[9] On the contrary, it the widest community we have. That is why the ICC, for all its faults, is so important.

8 | Postscript: the warrants

On 7 October 2005, the Ugandan defence minister, Amama Mbabazi, made an announcement in Kampala:

> The [ICC] investigation is complete and the court has taken a decision ... The following people have been indicted: Joseph Kony, Vincent Otti [LRA deputy commander-in-chief], Raska Lukwiya, Okot Odhiambo and Dominic Ongwen ... The warrants were served on Uganda for the government to execute the arrest order ... We have decided to cooperate with the court and we call upon the public to cooperate in the arrest of any of these named individuals.[1]

He explained that the governments of the Democratic Republic of the Congo (DRC) and Sudan had been served separately with arrest warrants for the five men, and that the Ugandan warrants had been passed on to Uganda's Director of Public Prosecutions in accordance with procedure. Mbabazi also noted that one of those 'indicted', Dominic Ongwen, had actually been killed in an engagement with Ugandan troops on 30 September.

Technically Mbabazi was not quite correct, the ICC does not 'indict', but moves directly to the issuing of warrants when judges in the pre-trial chamber accept an application from the Office of the Prosecutor (OTP). Also he had jumped the gun, because the existence of the warrants was still supposed to be a secret, although rumours about their existence had been circulating for some time.

It turned out that the OTP had actually made applications for warrants back in May 2005, but had requested that proceedings be under seal (i.e. kept secret) so that vulnerable groups would not be subject to risk of retaliatory attacks by the LRA, and so as not to undermine continuing investigative efforts. It was also requested that proceedings 'remain under seal until the security conditions in potentially affected areas improve or further measures can be arranged ...'[2] The judges sitting in the pre-trial chamber II of the ICC had accepted the request, and when the warrants were issued on 8 July 2005, that too was kept under seal. However, confidentiality was not sustained. As an Amnesty International media briefing put it, 'Unfortunately, certain persons who were informed of the existence of the warrants disclosed this information to the general public, thus increasing the risk that the accused will flee and dangers to victims and witnesses.'[3]

Interestingly, the initial leak does not appear to have come from the Ugandan government, but from the UN system – suggesting that the ICC's procedures are not as widely understood as they should be. At the end of September, the UN Under-Secretary General for Political Affairs, Ibrahim Gambari, told a news conference in Nairobi that the ICC had issued an arrest warrant for Kony.[4] Apparently, Gambari later said that he had 'misspoke', but by then other UN officials had confirmed that the warrant for Kony existed, and that there were also four others. The ICC at first refused to comment, but by the time Mbabazi made his announcement, there was little point in trying to maintain the fiction of confidentiality.

Any frustration about what had happened was kept well hidden by the court, and perhaps even suited the OTP. The OTP had made an application to the pre-trail chamber for the unsealing of warrants on 9 September, but the judges remained concerned about security issues. Following the initial leak in September, the OTP supplied the chamber with additional information on measures implemented for the protection of victims and witnesses. Taking this into account, and doubtless also the fact that information was already in the public domain, on 13 October

2005 the pre-trial chamber II decided formally to unseal the warrants.[5] The judges stated that they were:

> ... satisfied on the basis of the information provided ... that the overall plan in respect of the situation in Uganda for the security of witnesses and victims in the field has been completed and implemented; and that by the assessment and advice of the Prosecutor and the VWU [Victims and Witness Unit] this overall plan provides the necessary and adequate protective measures for all concerned at this stage.

Each warrant refers to the OTP's general allegations that the LRA has: 'engaged in a cycle of violence and established a pattern of "brutalization of civilians"'.[6] They also mention sources indicated by the prosecutor as confirming the roles of the accused, including 'statements from former LRA commanders, victims or witness accounts, radio broadcast recordings and short-wave radio LRA communications as intercepted by Ugandan investigative authorities ...' They then go on to list alleged crimes perpetrated by 'the key members of "Control Altar", the section representing the core LRA leadership', for which they are held to be individually responsible. These refer to six attacks that have been the focus of the OTP's investigation and, according to Chief Prosecutor Mareno-Ocampo, are 'some of the gravest attacks on civilians which the LRA has carried out in Northern Uganda since July 2002'.[7] Details of the alleged crimes are outlined, but with important details having been removed ('redacted') in the public versions.

The warrant for Joseph Kony lists twelve counts of crimes against humanity. He faces one count of sexual enslavement, one count of rape, four of enslavement, two of inhumane acts and four of murder. The remaining twenty-one counts are all of war crimes: four of murder (possibly of the same murders as the four counts mentioned as crimes against humanity), one of inducing rape, three of cruel treatment, five of pillaging, six of attacks against a civilian populations, and two of enlisting children. The warrant for Vincent Otti is similar. It lists eleven counts of crimes against humanity and twenty-one counts of war crimes. Okot Odhiambo stands accused of two counts of crimes against humanity and eight counts of war crimes. Dominic Ongwen (who Mbabazi claims is already dead) faces three counts of crimes against humanity and four counts of war crimes, and Raska Lukwiya one count of crimes against humanity and three counts of war crimes.

Issuing its first ICC warrants was an important moment. For UN Secretary-General Kofi Annan, it would 'send a powerful signal around the world that those responsible for such crimes will be held accountable for their actions'.[8] The EU High Representative for Common Foreign and Security Policy, Javier Solana, hailed it as a 'historic decision ... which expresses the Court's wish to put an end to the impunity in a region that suffered so much from grave human rights violations'.

Human Rights Watch and Amnesty International were also positive, although they both drew attention to alleged 'abuses committed by the Ugandan army'.[9] According to a statement by Amnesty International: 'The decision by the Prosecutor to proceed with issuing arrest warrants and, in doing so, resisting calls to suspend the investigation in favour of further political negotiations sends a clear message that without justice, there can be no prospect of a lasting peace for the region ...'[10] Nevertheless, Ugandan government accountability for 'the massive forcible displacement of civilians and other crimes against humanity and war crimes' had been overlooked: 'The failure of the Prosecutor to seek arrest warrants against Ugandan government forces and their civilian superiors is a matter of deep concern because the Ugandan prosecutors have failed to investigate and prosecute such crimes during the 19-year conflict ...'

Predictably, those who had questioned the ICC intervention all along were equally citical of the apparent one-sidedness of the warrants, and also dismissive of high-falutin claims about justice being done for LRA actrocities.[11] When asked questions following his annoncement about the warrants on 7 October, Mbabazi explained that the Ugandan government shall 'continue to encourage Bigombe in her efforts to talk peace with the LRA ... and will treat the others [i.e. rebels for whom no warrants have been issued] as people we can hold talks with and who can benefit from the amnesty'. But those for whom warrants had been issued would 'not be treated the same as before the indictment'. If Kony returned to Uganda from southern Sudan, the Ugandan military would attempt to arrest him on home soil and, if possible, they would pursue him across the border. He noted that the Ugandan Army Commander, Lieutenant General Aronda Nyakairima, was currently in Sudan requesting permission for Ugandan troops to cross the 'red line' beyond which it was not permitted to operate on Sudanese territory. For some it just sounded like an excuse for a reinvigoration of the military option.

Archbishop Odama of Gulu Catholic archdiocese responded to Mbabazi's remarks with the observation that, 'This is like a blow to the peace process. The process of confidence-building has been moving well, but now the LRA will look at whoever gets in contact with them as an agent of the ICC.'[12] Writing at the end of 2005, Adam Branch argues that 'the arrest warrants exposed the ICC's betrayal of the very principles of justice and law upon which the global court is supposed to be based ... [T]he ICC intervention represents a blatant instrumentalization of international law by the Ugandan government, which has, via the criminalization of the LRA, acquired international legitimacy for its military campaign and its refusal to engage in peace talks.'[13]

Earlier in the year, Betty Bigombe had threatened to withdraw from mediation talks if warrants were issued, and made her disappointment clear: 'You can no longer talk to the LRA as before, the dynamics have changed ... There is no doubt I need to make some adjustments, but the situation has been made difficult by the warrant ...' In the event she has not withdrawn, returning to Gulu in mid-November 2005, and has continued to talk to some of the LRA commanders on the phone. But her room for manoeuvre is certainly more limited. When I had asked Sam Kolo about the ICC soon after his surrender, he told me that Bigombe had said she would sort out any problems. As Mbabazi indicated, however, impunity under the Ugandan Amnesty Act is no longer possible for those named in the warrants. Now that the warrants are issued, even the OTP has a very limited role. The warrants cannot be withdrawn. There may the possibility of arguing that prosecution would not be in the interests of justice in the pre-trial chamber, but it is hard to see how a strong case could be made that would not compromise the purpose of the court. Vincent Otti, who has been doing most of the talking for the LRA, is aware that things have changed and that Bigombe may not be able to deliver much. For this reason he has been ringing other people, trying to forge alternative links and gather information about what is happening. He has been particularly concerned to know about such things as his rights to defence counsel, if he does end up in The Hague.

For Peter Onega, who chairs the Ugandan Amnesty Commission, the decision by the ICC to issue the warrants was a disaster. In his view, far from driving a wedge between the LRA leadership and the rest of the movement, it will allow them to consolidate their position and stop others surrendering. 'I can tell you very few will come out ... ICC should have known and measured out all the consequences before they issued out the warrant ... Does the taking of only five people for prosecution in The Hague bring about reconciliation among the divided Acholi people?'[14]

The warrants clearly weaken his position. Even without them, however, the Amnesty Commission has come in for a great deal of criticism. The points made in the main text of this book, that the granting of amnesty has appeared to reward certain individuals for perpetrating violence, have been given greater weight by the increased provision of 'amnesty packages'. Moreover, there are still bottlenecks in the allocation of amnesty cards, and a continuing muddle about what 'amnesty' means. In a survey that my research team carried out in mid-2005 based on interviews with over 200 'formerly abducted people' who had passed through the official reception centre process, we found that only 25 per cent had even heard of the Amnesty Commission, let alone applied for an amnesty certificate, and most of those that had heard of it had very confused ideas about what role it played.[15] We also found little evidence that the amnesty was an important factor in encouraging LRA combatants to surrender. Only senior commanders and some middle-ranking officers considered it significant.

To make things even worse for the commission, Amnesty International has seized upon the contradictions in the legal status of the Ugandan Amnesty Act. In the statement made supporting the ICC warrants, Amnesty International also made the following points about crimes against humanity and war crimes.

> The government of Uganda, as a state party to the Rome Statute, must take immediate steps to end the impunity it has imposed on the country by bringing to justice thousands of others accused of such crimes, including Ugandan government forces and their civilian superiors ... Most of these crimes committed are covered by a national amnesty law adopted by the Ugandan government that prevents prosecutions in Ugandan courts, although amnesties for crimes against humanity and war crimes are prohibited under international law ... The ICC in addition to prosecuting the accused, has a major role to play in working to-

gether with the government of Uganda and other governments to ensure that national courts investigate and, where there is sufficient admissible evidence, prosecute all persons suspected of such crimes including members of Ugandan government forces and their civilian superiors. In particular, Uganda must revoke its unlawful national amnesty seeking to protect perpetrators of the worst possible crimes from justice and begin comprehensive national investigations and prosecutions as soon as possible.

The ICC has kept out of these discussions, and staff continue to sidestep the issue by saying that amnesties are strictly a matter for national judiciaries. But really this is another way of saying that there is a basis in international law for national amnesties to be ignored. As one OTP staff member put it, 'Our intervention can be reconciled with the amnesty. We ignore it, and in a way they sort of reinforce each other.' Nevertheless, the existing Ugandan amnesty is certainly incompatible with the incorporation of the Rome Statute of the ICC into Ugandan law (which has still not happened). It means that, in theory, the legal status of the ICC warrants might be challenged in Ugandan courts, although it is unlikely that any case against the warrants could be pursued without governmental support.[16] It is much more probable that the Amnesty Act will be revised, or will just be set aside when it raises difficulties.

Whatever the status of the Amnesty Commission, Onega's point about the LRA leadership consolidating their position in response to the warrants has been shared by others, notably staff of aid agencies working on the ground in the war zone. There were concerns that they would become targets for LRA attacks, and that there will also be more attacks on IDP camps. When I returned to the war zone for two weeks in early November 2005, fears about the effects of the warrants seemed to have been confirmed by reports of LRA activity, especially in Kitgum and Pader districts, and across the border in parts of southern Sudan. Relief agencies had curtailed their operations in northern Uganda in late October, following three ambushes of staff in which two people were killed and four injured. The UN operations had resumed on 1 November, but on the following day de-mining activities were suspended in southern Sudan by the Swiss Foundation for Mine Action after two of their workers were killed. On 5 November another NGO worker was killed in Sudan and his wife and driver seriously wounded. Then on 8 November, a British resident of Uganda was killed in an ambush inside the boundaries of the Murchison Falls National Park, to the south west of Gulu. At the same time, a document ostensibly from the LRA was circulated, claiming that aid workers were now being targeted. There were no further ambushes of aid workers and expatriates in the following weeks, but attacks on civilians continued. In the worst of these, a minibus full of people was attacked in daylight hours close to the town of Pader, killing at least twelve people.

Not surprisingly, these incidents have been seen by those who had opposed the ICC intervention as evidence that the warrants were a blunder. It is not at all clear, however, that they are the result of a coordinated strategy. When I spoke to senior army officers in November, they were sceptical that the LRA had a new policy. In their view, the attacks on expatriates were probably being made by groups of rebels who wanted to steal things, so that they would have something to live on when they surrender, and they thought that the killing on 8 November had not been intended. There was evidence that the main aim of the ambush had been theft, and it was not the first such robbery to have occurred in Murchison Falls Park. Speaking by a satellite phone, probably stolen from an aid agency vehicle in Sudan, Vincent Otti accepted that some of the incidents in Sudan were LRA actions, but categorically denied that there was a policy of attacking aid workers. He was encouraged to phone the BBC

World Service and make a statement. He did this at the end of the month, saying that he wanted to 'talk with the government of Uganda to end the rebellion, because now we fought for twenty years – we are ready for this talk from today'. He also told the BBC that he was willing to cooperate with the ICC, but added that government officials should also face justice at the same court because they 'were responsible for some of the crimes committed in northern Uganda.' Government officials, however, were not in pressed, saying that the rebels are 'just buying time to reorganize themselves'.[17]

The current situation in mid-December 2005 is that Otti is continuing to talk to various people, including those mediating on behalf of the Ugandan government.[18] He also now has a better understanding of what would be involved in a trial based in The Hague, including the fact that he would not face the death penalty and would have defence council. It is hard to know, however, the degree to which he still speaks for Joseph Kony. There continue to be occasional, relatively small-scale attacks by LRA groups in Uganda, much as there were before the warrants were issued, but there have been no more fatal ambushes of aid agency vehicles. The overall political situation in the country has become tense, following the arrest of the leader of the opposition in mid-November, and there have been growing criticism of President Musevini's human rights record.[19] There has also been pressure on the government to change its policies in the north.

The Human Rights Watch statement on the ICC warrants, like that of Amnesty International, emphasized the need to prosecute the UPDF and government officials, and it referred to a scathing report which had been published by the organization in September.[20] This had documented numerous extrajudicial killings, rapes, arbitrary detentions and assaults by government forces that had occurred during the preceding twelve months, and 'a climate of fear and intimidation which impedes accountability'.

Postscript

In combination with the publication of the WHO study on the mortality and morbidity rates in the camps in July 2005, the Human Rights Watch report had contributed to demands for a change. It has become more widely recognized that the IDP camp approach is not an acceptable response to LRA incursions, and has political as well as strategic motivations. The Ugandan government has of course not accepted the criticisms, and the Ministry of Health has sought to distance itself from the WHO mortality and morbidity survey results. Presedent Museveni, however, has publicly called for plans to close some of the camps (those in Lira district) as soon as possible.

Events in Sudan are more difficult to gauge. Groups of LRA are still active, and they have probably continued to receive support from factions in the Sudan government or the Sudanese army. But they do not appear to be in a position to organize major incursions into Uganda. International pressures have forced the Sudan government to allow the UPDF to move beyond previously set limits in Sudan, and to operate without always giving prior notice.[21] It is, of course, also having to deal with the prospect of ICC warrants for crimes perpetrated in Darfur, including the possibility of warrants being issued for senior government officials – so there are doubtless other reasons too why links may be cut with the LRA. As for the SPLA, far from the death of Garang leading to a collapse in the peace process, the organization's new leader, Salva Kir, has given the impression of being more committed to stopping ongoing armed conflicts on the south, and has been prepared to be more cooperative over security issues. As one of those involved in the negotiations put it to me, 'Frankly, the death of Garang has promoted stability in the south (i.e. southern Sudan) and improved the chances of peace. Kir is proving to be a better leader for the SPLA.' At the end of November, a memorandum of understanding was agreed between the government of Uganda, the SPLA and the government of Sudan to cooperation in the execution of warrants. The government of the DRC had already agreed to execute the warrants as well. So the LRA leadership may now be beginning to feel that a trial in The Hague is a realistic prospect.

From the point of view of the ICC, the situation in Uganda has turned out rather better than might have been expected a year ago. Staff at the court claim that the intervention has actually proceeded according to their 'plan B'. Once it became apparent that there were local complexities, they decided 'to allow the peace process to take shape'. The OTP was required to keep a low profile for the investigators to be able to operate, but it was decided that the registry too had to keep a low profile for the first year: 'It was a deliberate policy. We had intended to pull back if negotiations were completed. Now we are raising our profile.' Among other things, the ICC has published an information booklet, which was included in the Ugandan daily newspapers after the warrants were unsealed, and Chief Prosecutor Moreno-Ocampo has recorded a statement on the prosecutions, which has been broadcast on Mega Radio from Gulu.[22]

When asked about the absence of warrants for the Ugandan government, I was told by the OTP that: 'The UPDF has been investigated, but alleged crimes perpetrated by the Ugandan government were not grave enough to reach the threshold. We focus on the gravity of a crime.' I also asked about the choice and the protection of witnesses.

We have had no witnesses who have refused to testify. We have found that all victims want to say what has happened to them, and we have not found any differences in willingness to testify between the different groups. Acholis have been just as willing to testify as the others. We selected alleged crimes partly on their geographical distribution – including crimes in Acholi area ... The bulk of the witness protection comes before the trial. We

Postscript

have to make a careful assessment before making contact. We always have a psychologist with us, who makes an assessment before we proceed with an interview. When it comes to the court proceeding, witnesses can present in camera, and we certainly can preserve anonymity. We will never put a witness in jeopardy. We know exactly how we will protect witnesses, and we are confident that our witnesses are secure.

The judges in the pre-trial chamber, however, have their doubts. Towards the end of November a decision was made to convene a status conference, in a closed session, on matters related to safety and security in Uganda. This was done in response to: 'recent reports in the Ugandan and international media on serious attacks and violence against civilians in northern Uganda and southern Sudan, allegedly by the Lord's Resistance Army, resulting in the death of at least twenty-two civilians, including humanitarian workers, as well as in a significant number of injuries and abductions ...' The judges had concerns 'about the impact of such serious attacks and violence may have (1) on the overall plan for safety and security of victims and witnesses and (2) on the security of the Court in the field ...'[23]

It is also important to reiterate that if the accused do end up in court, there will be cases prepared for the defence, and protection of defence witnesses may prove to be more difficult than protection of those for the prosecution, particularly in the light of current political developments, which have included threats to the Ugandan judiciary. If proceedings in The Hague look as if they might be embarrassing or worse for the government, defence witnesses may well be vulnerable (as senior army officers based in Gulu told me a year ago when I explained the court process to them). At the same time, pressures may increase on the OTP both from donors and from within the ICC system to come up with arrest warrants for government representatives.

Forcible displacement of population is a war crime under the Rome Statute, and it has obviously occurred on a massive scale. It is hard to see how it lacks gravity. It may be difficult to find enough evidence with which to hold individuals accountable but, according to the text of another decision made in the pre-trial chamber in early December, 'OTP investigations and assessments of allegations made against the military forces of the Government of Uganda are ongoing.'[24] There is also the possibility that the Security Council will pass a resolution critical of the Ugandan government.[25]

As far as holding the LRA high command to account is concerned, now that warrants are unsealed, the initiative has passed from the OTP to the states parties who are required to execute them. There are signs that measures are being put in place to do that, possibly including the deployment of 'special forces'. The role of the USA in these events is unclear, and efforts will probably be made to keep any support for the execution of the warrants secret. The USA is, however, interested in spending substantial funds on the reconstruction of southern Sudan and in increasing assistance to northern Uganda. The Bush administration has also had to adjust its outright antipathy to the ICC since the Security Council referral of Darfur and, as has been mentioned, the State Department has played a role in brokering security collaboration between the SPLA and the governments of Uganda and Sudan.[26] Whatever plans are being made, the ICC needs things to move on quickly. Many analysts and activists have argued that the introduction of international criminal justice has already been an obstacle to peace. I have disagreed. But it may become so if the warrants are seen to lack credibility and LRA commanders retain a capacity to initiate violent acts. It will not be long before those interested in establishing political order look for ways of sidelining the court. For the ICC, the clock is now ticking.[27]

Notes

1 Introduction

1 'President of Uganda refers situation concerning the Lord's Resistance Army (LRA) to the ICC', press release, International Criminal Court, The Hague, 29 January 2004.

2 Apparently the delegation from Andorra wanted it to state that international crimes 'rip asunder the delicate tapestry' that keeps humankind together, but the Japanese complained that the concept of a tapestry was not widely known in their country. Replacing it with a shattered mosaic perhaps reflected the fact that the meeting was being held in Rome (Sands 2005: 55).

3 It is revealing that one of the most insightful and widely read books dealing with the ICC (Sands 2005) fails to mention this fact. Darfur had not been referred at the time he was writing it, but the other three investigations were already under way. Not surprisingly, staff at the ICC deny that political considerations are a factor. They maintain that prosecutions are purely related to the gravity of the alleged offence.

4 The ICC's Office of the Prosecutor had been investigating the situation in the Congo without a state party reference since July 2002 at the behest of individuals and NGOs.

5 The ICC prosecutor quickly made a public statement to the effect that this incident would fall under the jurisdiction of the ICC ('Statement by the Prosecutor related to crimes committed in Barlonya camp in Uganda', press release, ICC, The Hague, 23 February 2004).

6 Some international lawyers would disagree. For Rosalyn Higgins, currently a judge at the International Court of Justice, international law is the interlocking of power with authority (made up of accumulated past legal decisions combined with the interpretations of judicial specialists and institutions). On the one hand, authority cannot exist in the total absence of control. On the other, when power overrides authority it is not lawful (Higgins 1994: 4). It is a perspective that has the merit of being based in experience, but it begs the question of who decides when actions are unlawful, and with what consequences.

7 Churchill had wanted to execute the leading Nazis without any judicial process, but was prevailed upon by the USA to accept that they should be given fair trials.

8 Quoted in Robertson (2000: 36). The ambassador himself was an architect of Stalin's show trials.

9 Examples include the International Covenant on Civil and Political Rights and the International Covenant on Economic and Social Rights. The USA did not actually ratify the Genocide Convention until 1988.

10 In most respects, Security Council Resolution 955, which established the ICTR, followed the example set in Resolutions 808 and 827, although it restricted jurisdiction to the events of 1994 (i.e. the year of the genocide), whereas the ICTY was mandated to investigate crimes occurring since 1991.

11 Until 2003 the ICTR shared the same prosecutor and appeals chamber as the ICTY in the Netherlands, but most of its hearings have taken place in Arusha. Tanzania was the one African country that had in the past responded vigorously to crimes against humanity occurring in a neighbouring state. So in one way this was an appropriate choice. It has, however, made the ICTR a remote affair for most Rwandans and acutely limited any sense of ownership of the proceedings.

12 For a good general discussion of the ICTR, see des Forges and Longman (2004). In former Yugoslavia there have also been bitter complaints about the Hague Tribunal's relationship with national judiciaries. For the ICTY, however, there has been much more involvement through its 'rules of the road' programme, whereby the ICTY's Office of the Prosecutor reviews evidence from national courts before allowing the issuing of local warrants. Whatever the intention, an effect of these measures has been to exacerbate tensions between international and national judicial processes. For a good discussion of these issues, see Fletcher and Weinstein (2004).

13 A Spanish magistrate had issued an order for his arrest for crimes of genocide and terrorism. After protracted hearings in British courts, the House of Lords ordered his extradition to Spain to face charges of torture in November 1998 and again in October 1999. In the event, the British government arranged for him to be returned to Chile in 2000 – ostensibly for health reasons. But while he may have escaped a criminal trial, his detention revealed that apparently arcane points of international law can have real weight within domestic legal processes.

14 The overlapping definitions of crimes against humanity and war crimes is a problem in international criminal law. It results in the practice of jointly charging for both crimes. It has raised the question: Is it possible for one offence to be characterized as two crimes? The problem has been seriously compounded in the Rome Statute of the ICC. See Jia (1999). However, staff at the ICC claim that in practice it will not present significant difficulties.

15 Concerns about prosecution of peacekeepers has been the publicly expressed reason for opposing the ICC, but probably there are equal concerns about the court prosecuting someone like Henry Kissinger or Donald Rumsfeld for command responsibility. The chances of this happening too, however, are minimal. Although it is unlikely that such people will ever be prosecuted within the USA, a state party or Security Council referral would be unthinkable. The ICC prosecutor could still launch an investigation, but to what purpose? Even if a convincing case could be made to the Pre-Trial Chamber, it would be impossible to serve the warrants.

16 US Terrorist Exclusion List under Section 411 of the USA Patriot Act of 2001, 8 USC se. 1882.

17 See Sands (2005).

18 In January 2005, a reliable informant told me that the court was in fact receiving quite a bit of cooperation from the US government.

19 From a statement by the Hungarian ambassador to the UN during the Security Council debate before the vote to create the ICTY. Quoted in Fletcher and Weinstein (2004: 36).

20 Antonio Cassese, quoted in Stover and Weinstein (2004: 3).

21 Branch (2004: 5).

2 The coming of the Lord's Resistance Army

1 Early accounts of the area that has come to be known as Acholiland use a variety of tribal labels for the groups that lived there. The terms Shuli (or Shooli) and Gangi were the most common. The former may have been derived from Shilluk, a people living in Sudan who also speak Lwo. The latter seems to have been connected with the Lwo word for 'home'. An early usage of Acholi comes from the end of the nineteenth century. One British officer claimed that the people were called Choli or Acholi in the plural. This suggests a link with the Lwo word for 'black'. Another possibility is that the term Acholi may have been derived from the Lwo for a person (*laco*). In any case, the term Acholi did not enter into general usage until the second decade of the twentieth century.

2 'Panorama asks if the first genocide of the 21st century is occurring in Darfur', BBC News, 14 November 2004 (<news.bbc.co.uk/2/hi/ programmes/panorama/4006837.stm>). A recent report produced in response to a UN Security Council resolution on Darfur (SCR 1564) has concluded that genocide has not been perpetrated, but that serious crimes against humanity and war crimes have occurred. It strongly recommends that the Security Council immediately refer the situation of

Darfur to the ICC. 'Report of the International Commission on Darfur to the UN Secretary-General', 25 January 2005 (<www.un.org/News/dh/sudan/com_inq_darfur.pdf>). The USA opposed this move, and continued to claim that genocide had occurred. 'US convinced of Darfur "genocide"', BBC News <news.bbc.co.uk/1/hi/world/africa/4227835.stm>. The Bush administration, however, was eventually forced to back down.

3 It has become established as a paradigm for explaining why institutions of governance in Africa fail, and how international assistance merely compounds the problems. See, for example, Harrell-Bond (1986); Keen (1994); de Waal (1997).

4 Bayart et al. (1999: 5).

5 The number of Acholi in the UNLA is a sensitive issue. It has become common to use 'Acholi' as a shorthand for all those alleged to have killed civilians in Luwero. When I visited Uganda in the early 1980s, however, I found that many of the soldiers I met were not from the north at all, and those that were did not necessarily speak Lwo. It is impossible to make an accurate assessment, but it is likely that the number of northerners in the UNLA was initially less than 40 per cent and then subsequently rose to over 60 per cent. Acholi certainly became the dominant group following Okello's coup in 1985.

6 The literature on this issue is substantial. It dates back to the great study by E. E. Evans-Pritchard (1937). For recent reviews and discussion of insights from such work and how it relates to northern Uganda, see Allen (2000).

7 A fascinating and very readable account of these developments is p'Bitek (1971).

8 For discussion of witch-hunts in Uganda during the 1960s, see Abrahams (1985); and Heald (1989). For a discussion of more recent attacks on 'witches' in northern Uganda – in this case encouraged by the local Catholic Church – see Allen (1991a, 1992, 1999a).

9 According to Alice, an UNLA commander called Bajilo Lara had approached her and asked for spiritual assistance, because Obote planned to 'get rid of all Acholi big men'. Alice's spirit then told the envoy: 'This is a holy war: when you stop killing and looting civilians, I will help you. However, if you will not obey the Holy Spirit order after the take-over you will be removed after six months and a lot of people will die for the sake of your evil.' She also claimed that Okello would still be in power if he had correctly fulfilled the mission. From an interview with Robert Schlenker, 27 August 1999, quoted in Schlenker (1999: 15–16).

10 Alice herself is sometimes called the Lakwena. Interestingly,

at the 1994 peace talks Joseph Kony was referred to as *laoor* by the
Ugandan minister of state, Betty Bigombe. This is another Lwo term for
messenger, but perhaps with less explicit biblical associations. Showing
Kony respect in this way helps explain the LRA's willingness to speak to
her both in 1994 and again ten years later.

11 It is a remarkable place, located on a rock in the Nile below the
Murchison Falls.

12 The main studies of Alice Lakwena and the Holy Spirit Movement are Allen (1991b); and Behrend (1999).

13 Schlenker (1999: 16).

14 Outside Acholiland, some former UPDA soldiers and also some
of the remnants of the HSMF joined the Uganda People's Democratic
Army. This was a movement fighting the government in the Teso area.

15 According to Alice's own account, it was the Lakwena spirit
which instructed her to become Catholic. She claims, however, not
to have actually changed her religion, and has not yet seen a Catholic
church from the inside. From an interview with Robert Schlenker,
27 August 1999, quoted in Schlenker (1999: 26).

16 Apparently she is demanding more money before returning.
She has also written to one of those in contact with her stating that the
Acholi are 'very stupid people', and that she will not return to live in the
Acholi area (personal communication with an informant in Gulu town,
November 2004).

17 According to information sent to me by Filipo Ciantia, the
maternal grandfather of Alice and Kony was a man named Okello
Kallisa. His two daughters were Aya, the mother of Alice, and Nora
Oling, the mother of Kony.

18 Sverker Finnstom has informed me that one of his informants
told him about meetings between Alice and Kony in Sudan. Apparently
in recent years they have developed a good relationship and discussed
tactics (personal communication, 7 February 2005). I have no confirma-
tion of this.

19 It is has sometimes been reported that he nominally converted
to Islam in Sudan, but none of our informants confirmed this.

20 The most important published work on the LRA and the effects
of continuous war in Acholiland is Finnstrom (2003). This is an
outstanding ethnographic account. Another fascinating study is Dolan
(2005). This presents a great deal of detailed information about the
LRA, and is available as a LSE PhD thesis. A shorter recent overview of
the war, mainly based on newspaper articles and secondary sources, is
van Acket (2004). Other useful articles and reports include: Doom and

Vlassenroot (1999); Gersony (1997); Lomo and Hovil (2004); Lucima (2002).

21 Gersony (1997: 35).

22 Quoted in Nyeko and Lucima (2002). For an excellent discussion of the LRA manifestos, see Finnstrom (2003: ch. 4).

23 I am grateful to Chris Dolan for drawing this development to my attention. Details given here about Radio Free Uganda and Radio Mega are taken from Chris Dolan's forthcoming LSE PhD thesis.

24 A Northern Uganda Reconstruction Programme was set in motion at the time, with World Bank assistance. Only a small percentage of the budget was actually spent, however.

25 Other accounts have mentioned only two meetings, but Bigombe herself has told me that she met Kony five times. They built up a relationship which has proved important in more recent negotiations.

26 This is one reason why the government of Uganda has persistently claimed that the LRA has no coherent political agenda.

27 Government officials and army officers often make a similar claim about the LRA. At a meeting at the Acholi Inn in Gulu in November 2004, a group of senior UPDF officers told me that the war was mainly due to Kony and his commanders benefiting economically from the situation. It is the case that Kony and his commanders enjoyed many benefits from the association with the Sudan government, including sophisticated military equipment, cars, radios and various other items. It should be added that the Acholi Inn is the best hotel in Gulu and is currently being renovated and expanded. It is also owned by the family of one of the UPDF officers who were present at the meeting.

28 De Temmerman (2001).

29 For example, Branch (2004).

3 Displacement and abduction

1 These figures are from WFP and UNOCHA sources and are quoted in Dolan (1995).

2 To give just one example, in 2005 some expatriates who had rented a house in Gulu town opened a locked door to one of the rooms. They found a girl of about fourteen. The house had previously been rented to some students, who had left that morning. They had been keeping her in the room in return for sex. One study that has highlighted the plight of girls in northern Uganda is McKay and Mazurana (2004).

3 Falk et al. (2004).

4 MSF-Holland (2004a).

5 These data are based on anthropometric assessments. The findings from such surveys are useful, but can be very misleading if they are
not linked to mortality assessments. Malnutrition figures of the levels
found in camps in Pader and Lira might indicate an 'acceptable' situation, in that similar levels are found in other places. This may, however,
disguise the number of children who are dying. A high mortality rate
for small children will mean that more food is available for those who
survive. From the mortality data collected by MSF-Holland, that would
appear to be the case in this instance.

6 WHO (2005).

7 MSF-Holland (2004b).

8 Detailed accounts of such abuses appear, for example, in the
works of Dolan (2005) and Finnstrom (2003), and in the reports of
human rights agencies. The official report submitted to the US Congress under the Northern Uganda Crisis Act in February 2005 noted
that 'The number of reports ... show [*sic*] that gender-based crime is a
significant problem, and there is persuasive anecdotal and case-specific
evidence of involvement by members of the security forces.' Such statements have made the UPDF very sensitive about the issue. Following
the release of the report on sexual and gender-based violence in Pabbo
camp (cited below), a team of senior army officers were sent to the
region to investigate.

9 One of many recent report assuming high rates of HIV/Aids in
northern Uganda is Akuma et al. (2005). The WHO mortality survey of
2005 found that Aids was the second-most common self-reported cause
of death in Gulu, Kitgum and Pader districts (13.5 per cent).

10 Ugandan HIV prevalence rates based on antenatal surveillance
are available in *STD/HIV/AIDS Surveillance Report*, STD/AIDS Control
Programme, Ministry of Health, Kampala, June 2003 <www.health.
go.ug/docs/hiv0603.pdf>. No population surveys have been attempted
in northern Uganda, so there are no assessments of HIV incidence rates
(i.e. rates of new infection). Antenatal surveillance data are relatively
easy to collect, but may be misleading, for two main reasons: first, many
women in Uganda do not attend antenatal clinics and those who do
may be a self-selecting sample of urban or peri-urban residents; second,
an effect of HIV is to reduce fertility, so women who are HIV positive are
less likely to become pregnant. For a critical commentary on the various
claims that have been made about the Ugandan data, see Allen and
Heald (2004) and Allen (2006).

11 Ciantia (2004).

12 Women selected as 'wives' are mostly very young and often

attending school at the time of their abduction. One informant explained to us that older women are sometimes used as servants rather than for sexual purposes. She told us that she was not given to any of the LRA soldiers as a 'wife' because the senior commanders said that she might be infected with HIV/Aids (after her escape, she found that she had a venereal disease).

13 World Vision (2004: 28).

14 A report that stresses a link between the Ugandan army and the spread of HIV/Aids is Dolan and Bagenda (2004). For a detailed discussion of the effect of war on HIV rates in Uganda, see Allen (2006).

15 World Vision, like most of the other reception centres, has not systematically tested those who have been abducted for HIV. One reception centre based in Lira town, however, has arranged HIV tests for almost all those who have passed through it and are assessed as having been at risk of infection (notably women who have returned with children). There has been only one confirmed case of HIV.

16 For an interview with Carol Bellamy soon after her visit to northern Uganda in May 2004, see <www.irinnews.org/report.asp?ReportID=4 1346&SelectRegion=East_Africa&SelectCountry=UGANDA>.

17 In Sudan, analysts have claimed that aid has been imposed, that agencies have fuelled armed conflict, and that the 'humanitarian international' has perpetrated famine crimes. Such critiques have led to a crisis of confidence among many aid workers, or, as David Reiff puts it, a crisis of conscience – see Reiff (2002). Here are some remarks Reiff made at a recent talk to the Carnegie Council: 'For a long time, humanitarians who were criticized were in denial about the down side, the unintended negative consequences of their actions ... But as time went on, it became clear that they were their own failures ... Some twenty-odd years ago it was decided to make a permanent humanitarian operation, a consortium of most of the mainline humanitarian agencies under UN auspices, called Operation Lifeline Sudan (OLS) ... The trouble is that as humanitarians themselves, they realized before long that they were becoming logisticians to the war effort of the belligerents, that in effect what Operation Lifeline Sudan was doing, whilst doing a great deal of good by saving lives, the humanitarians were in effect allowing the war to continue, because both the Government of Sudan, and the then two major insurgent groups in the south ... were saying, "Okay, you are our social service arm. The people are hungry. Surely you, United Nations and OLS, will feed these folks. And we, whilst you are feeding them, will go about our merry way, slaughtering each other, and, incidentally, quite a few of these civilians you are trying to feed while we are at it." There was a crisis of conscience among sensible humanitarian

agencies' (<www.carnegiecouncil.org/viewMedia.php/prmID/169>). One of the most devastating critiques of humanitarian aid to Sudan, including OLS, is de Waal (1997). A good recent overview of the debates is Johnson (2003).

18 It might also be noted that the Ugandan army sometimes makes people do certain kinds of work, such as cutting grass near the roads. This may not be experienced as so different from some 'abductions' by the LRA.

19 ICTJ and HRC (2005).

20 UNICEF (2001).

21 FAFO (2005).

22 WHO (2005).

23 World Vision claims that 10,000 children were abducted in 2002 alone (World Vision 2004: 37). It is not clear, however, where the data for this figure come from. They were not collected by World Vision staff in Gulu. Nor is it known how many of those abducted since 2002 are still with the LRA. Data from reception centres from 2003–05 suggest that most of those returning had been abducted recently. Using similar statistics from the GUSCO and World Vision reception centres in Gulu up to early 2002, Chris Dolan has argued that the rate of reintegration of children abducted by the LRA is at least 88 per cent. He concludes that, as of early 2002, the number of children remaining with the LRA was 'at the very most around 900' (Dolan 2002). Recently, UNICEF has reported that during 2003 and 2004 a total of 15,000 persons, most of them children, were recorded as abducted (<www.reliefweb.int/library/documents/2004/unicef-uga-22dec.pdf>). It is again not clear, however, how accurate these data are, or where they have come from. The figure appears to have been made up in New York, and there seems to have been no consultation with local staff. In a personal communication, the head of child protection for UNICEF Kampala has suggested a figure of 12,000 abductions for 2004 and 2003, but accepts that this is a guess. It is not known how many have been children, or how many remain with the LRA. It is likely, however, that the number of children still missing and not dead is less than 2,000 and is possibly less than 1,000 (personal communications with Andrew Mawson, 3 and 5 February 2005).

24 'Background information on the situation in Uganda', ICC press release, 29 January 2004 <www.icc-cpi.int/library/press/pressreleases/Uganda_200401_EN.doc>.

25 IRIN interview with UN Under-Secretary Mr Jan Egeland, 12 November 2003, quoted in the *SCiU Statement on ICC Prosecution of LRA*, February 2004. Egeland's comments echo the terms used by some local activists who refer to 'our children in the bush'. In northern

Uganda a person tends to be viewed as 'like a child' until he or she has reproduced.

26 The literature on the use of terror in wars since the early 1990s is substantial. Two key books are Kaldor (1999) and Duffield (2001). For a general overview, see Allen (1999b).

27 According to UNICEF data, the ADF abducted 1,292 people between 1996 and 2001, of whom 612 were children (UNICEF 2001).

28 Some of the men who have been given 'wives' have had no choice other than to accept them. Some former LRA combatants reported that their sex life was monitored, and that they would receive 'medical' treatment if they failed to impregnate their 'wife'. There are also reports that women who did not conceive were punished.

29 The person killed could be a woman as well as a man. See Girling (1960: 103).

4 Amnesty, peace talks and prosecution

1 The quotes in this paragraph are taken from *The Monitor* newspaper. They are also cited in Makerere University's Refugee Law Project position statement on the ICC, 28 July 2004.

2 US Congress, PL 108-283.

3 The Amnesty Act applies to 'war and armed rebellion', while the Terrorism Act refers to violence used 'indiscriminately without due regard to the safety of others or property'. It seems that the crucial issue is that of the intention of the accused. For a useful discussion of this point, see Lomo and Hovil (2004: 45–6).

4 'Ceasefire extended into Sudan', *New Vision*, 15 December 2004. There has not been much comment on this extension of the ceasefire to Sudan, but it is a remarkable incident. It has involved one sovereign state openly offering a ceasefire to a non-governmental military group within the territory of another state and without any reference to the government of that state.

5 'President of Uganda refers situation concerning the Lord's Resistance Army (LRA) to the ICC', press statement, The Hague, 29 January 2004.

6 Amnesty International, public statement AFR 59/001/2004, 30 January 2004.

7 UNOCHA coverage of the SCiU statement can be found at <www.relifweb.int/rw/rwb.nsf/AllDocsByUNID/c1290f89727275fac1256e3c005956eb>.

8 See, for example, the position paper of the Refugee Law Project, Faculty of Law, Makerere University, 28 July 2004, p. 5 <www.

refugeelawproject.org>. The situation in the Congo had not yet been referred to the ICC by the government of Congo at the time of the Ugandan referral, but Chief Prosecutor Moreno-Ocampo had been carrying out an investigation under his own powers since mid-2002.

9 Makerere University's Refugee Law Project statement on the ICC intervention in northern Uganda, 5 August 2004 <http://www.hrea. org/lists/refugee-rights/markup/msg00503.html>. The complete position paper, from which the statement is taken, is available at <www. refugeelawproject.org>. The working paper mentioned in the statement can be found at <http://www.refugeelawproject.org/working%20papers/ RLP%20WP11%20Northern%20Uganda.pdf>.

10 Father Carlos Rodriguez, public statement, quoted in Branch (2004). The previous quote by Bishop Mcleod Ochola is also cited in the above article.

11 'Suggestions by the Acholi religious and cultural leaders in response to the request by the International Criminal Court', statement, Gulu, 12 November 2004.

12 In January, staff at the ICC told me that there were plans for the Registry to become more actively engaged in outreach work from February 2005. But this did not happen. In March and April 2005, however, delegations from northern Uganda went to The Hague and made joint public statements with the ICC. This development is discussed in Chapter 7.

13 I am particularly grateful to Mariana Goetz and Christine Chinkin of the London School of Economics for providing me with details of comparison between the ICC and the SCSL, ICTY and ICTR.

14 The USA has not taken such an extreme line on all discussions in the Security Council and (according to staff at the ICC) in practice some US government officials have been more supportive of the ICC than public discourse suggests. The main concern of the current US administration is that US troops involved in peacekeeping missions are not liable to prosecution. For a review of US policy on the ICC, see the website of the American Non-Governmental Organizations Coalition for the International Criminal Court. An excellent discussion about the tensions over US peacekeeping forces can found at <http://www.amicc.org/ usinfo/administration_policy_pkeeping.html>. A recent compromise in the Security Council relates to Resolution 1565 of 1 October 2004, which extends the United Nations mission in the Democratic Republic of Congo until March 2005. Article 5(g) states that the mission will have a mandate 'to assist in the promotion and protection of human rights, with particular attention to women, children and vulnerable persons, investigate human rights violations to put an end to impunity, and con-

tinue to cooperate with efforts to ensure that those responsible for serious violations of human rights and international humanitarian law are brought to justice, while working closely with the relevant agencies of the United Nations'. The United States supported Resolution 1565 with the understanding that it did not direct the UN mission to cooperate with the ICC, and that any expenses resulting from the provision of any cooperation or support to the ICC would need to be on a reimbursable basis. Thus, although the ICC is not mentioned in the resolution, the possibility of cooperation in the Congo is not precluded.

15 As far as the ICC is concerned, domestic amnesties are strictly a matter for national authorities, and do not prevent the exercise of the ICC's jurisdiction. Nevertheless, in practice the ICC depends on state parties for cooperation. So this problem cannot simply be ignored.

16 Staff at the ICC have confirmed that there was an interest in the case before the referral. There was also considerable lobbying of the government of Uganda by some concerned organizations to ensure that a referral occurred.

17 State parties are those states that have ratified the Rome Statute of the ICC. As explained elsewhere, the ICC is a treaty-based court and does not have its own mechanisms of enforcement. It has to rely on the cooperation of state parties.

18 Ratified by Sudan in 1990.

19 'Report of the International Commission on Darfur to the UN Secretary-General', 25 January 2005 <www.un.org/News/dh/sudan/com_inq_darfur.pdf>.

20 Citizens for Global Solutions (2004). It is possible that the Ugandan government told the ICC that the war was over and that the problem was a matter of border violations by criminals. Also, at the time of the referral, much of the Equatoria Defence Force had been incorporated into the SPLA as part of the Sudan peace arrangements. It might have been anticipated that this would end effective support for the LRA in Sudan and isolate the LRA leadership. This may now have happened, but has taken longer than expected.

21 There are two other possible ways in which the ICC intervention in northern Uganda might theoretically be stopped. One involves the intervention of the UN Security Council under Article 12 of the Rome Statute; another is that the Ugandan government decides to try the LRA commanders itself. Neither is likely to happen. For a useful discussion of these issues, see CSOPNU (2005).

22 'Court rules out Kony immunity', *New Vision*, 18 April 2005.

23 According to media reports, this has been stated on a number of occasions by President Museveni, army officers and members of the

207

government. A recent example was reported in *New Vision* on 5 January 2005: 'Govt can withdraw ICC case, says army'.

24 Afako (2004); Citizens for Global Solutions (2004); SCiU (2004a, 2004b); Branch (2004).

5 Concerns about the court

1 Amnesty International, public statement AFR 59/001/2004.

2 Letter to President Kirsch, dated 17 June 2004, Office of the Prosecutor, International Criminal Court, ICC-02/04-1 06-07-2004 4/4 UN.

3 Branch (2004).

4 Conversation with Barney Afako, 13 November 2004. Other legal experts have taken the view that it would be possible, provided that the cases are discrete.

5 It is the policy of the Office of the Prosecutor to avoid using government vehicles, but it may have happened, and this policy does not apply to other parts of the ICC. Rumours about the Office of the Prosecutor using government officials to lever access were confirmed by informants in one case.

6 This was confirmed by ICC staff at a meeting in The Hague in January 2005.

7 'Background information on the situation in Uganda', ICC press release, 29 November 2004 <www.icc-cpi.int/library/press/pressreleases/Uganda_200401_EN.doc>.

8 A suggestion that has been made by some local activists in northern Uganda is that there should be a truth commission first, and then those most responsible for atrocities could be tried later. But it is hard to see how this could work. Truth commissions tend to provide impunity for those who testify. If those found to have perpetrated the worst crimes were put forward for prosecution, there would be no incentive for alleged perpetrators of atrocities to participate (or tell the truth). With the setting up of the ICC, those alleged to be most responsible will probably have to be arrested before a truth commission is set up. The remainder might then be given some form of impunity (although the ICC would still have jurisdiction to ignore it). As the court becomes more active, this may be a far-reaching implication of the ratification of the Rome Treaty, at least for state parties.

9 Similar events have been reported in Lira district. It is worth noting that during the 1990s guerrilla groups operating in north-west Uganda, notably the West Nile Bank Front, were linked with the LRA through the Sudan government. A few people from the north-west became LRA commanders. I have not, however, heard of any of them being Madi.

10 Branch (2004).

11 Afako (2004).

12 Rome Statute of the International Criminal Court, 1998, Article 68, Clause 5.

13 'Background information on the situation in Uganda', op. cit. The ICC is not alone. Similar information is presented in many other statements and reports – for example, World Vision, *Pawns of Politics: Children, Conflict and Peace in Northern Uganda*, Washington, DC, 2004.

14 The ICC background information document of January 2004 does implicitly suggest that the government of Uganda as well as the LRA might be held to account for 'conscription' of children under fifteen. The scale of recruitment of children into the Ugandan armed forces is unknown. It is also important to note that recruitment into the formal armed forces of children aged fifteen to seventeen occurs in several countries, including the UK, and is not a crime under the ICC statute.

15 See Nyeko and Lucima (2002).

16 At the time this did not seem very likely to me, but that was before the referral of Darfur to the ICC.

17 She had apparently assured him that she could protect him from any possible prosecution.

18 A good discussion of these issues is in Afako (2004: 3–6).

19 Refugee Law Project (2004: 7).

20 She will not, however, have been given a guarantee of this by the Office of the Prosecutor.

21 This interview with Kenneth Banya was conducted by Mikkel Dalum in November 2004.

22 For an interesting discussion of this incident, see Joseph K. Tellewoyan, 'Analysis of the indictment of President Charles Taylor of Liberia by the Special Court for Sierra Leone', available at <http://pages.prodigy.net/jkess3/CharlesTaylor2.htm>.

23 ICTJ and HRC (2005).

24 The number of respondents wanting punishment for the LRA was lowest in Gulu district (44 per cent) and highest in Lira district (88 per cent).

25 Human Rights Focus, *The Examiner*, issue 1, Gulu, 2005.

6 *Justice and healing*

1 Branch (2004: 5), quoted at the end of Chapter 1.

2 ICC paper on some policy issues before the Office of the Prosecu-

tor, ICC-OTP, September 2003 (available at <www.icc-cpi.int/otp/otp_
policy.html>), pp. 2 and 5. The paper also notes on p. 5 that 'the many
implications of the principle of complementarity and the lack of court
rulings' means that 'detailed, exhaustive guidelines for its operation
will probably be developed over the years'.

3 Lomo and Hovil (2004: 45). Many otherwise thoughtful and well-
informed contributions continue to assert this view without serious
question. For example, on 1 February 2005 the Civil Society for Peace
in Northern Uganda issued a briefing paper. It contains the following
statement on 'traditional justice mechanisms in Acholi': 'It is worth
mentioning a few words about the Acholi justice system, which is based
on compensation, reconciliation and reintegration. The main objective
of the justice system is to integrate perpetrators into their communities
with their victims, through a process of establishing the truth, confession, reparation, repentance and forgiveness. Mechanisms such as
mato oput and *bending of the spears* are ancient Acholi rituals which,
despite many years of war and displacement, are still being practised in
the sub-region, and have the support and confidence of the majority of
Acholis and their traditional leaders ...'. CSOPNU, c/o CARE, Kampala,
Uganda, e-mail <csopnu@yahoo.com>.

4 Marc Lacey, 'Atrocity victims in Uganda choose to forgive', *New
York Times*, 18 April 2005 (available at <www.globalpolicy.org/intljustice/
icc/2005/0418forgive.htm>).

5 An important exception is the recent questionnaire-based study
by the ICTJ and HRC (2005).

6 For example, 'Suggestions by the Acholi religious and cultural
leaders in response to the request by the International Criminal Court',
press release, 12 November 2004; and 'Joint press statement by the
cultural and religious leaders', ARLPI, 15 November 2004, which deals
with the peace talks and is signed by both Archbishop Odama and
Paramount Chief Acana II.

7 Pain (1997).

8 He had at one time been a schoolteacher in Gulu town (on
which he wrote a PhD thesis) and had worked for Oxfam in Uganda
in the 1980s. He makes his point of view clear from the start of the
report. On the title page, Pain writes *'Lacwec tye!'* (which means 'The
Creator is present!'), and he dedicates the report to 'the one who has
inspired it and is alone responsible for creating the consensus which
it represents'. He goes on to state that he had been a close friend
of Archbishop Janani Luwum, whom he calls 'one of Uganda's and
Acholi's greatest leaders'. Luwum had been one of the most prominent
figures in the Anglican Church to become a Balokole (see Chapter 2 and

below). He was murdered by Amin in 1977 and has a kind of mythical status among some Acholi. The spirit of Luwum is reported to have been one of twelve spirits that possessed a woman called Poline Angom in 1987. She was one of Joseph Kony's followers, and Kony allowed her to work in one of his 'yards' (Behrend 1999: 186–7).

9 'Acholi chief opposes Kony trial', *New Vision*, 8 November 2004.

10 A recent report by the Catholic aid agency Caritas recognizes this. It noted that *mato oput* is used in a 'metaphorical' way to refer to any process of reconciliation. It has been 'romanticized and idealized as if it was a kind of magic bullet to solve any kind of conflict' (Caritas 2005: 12).

11 ICTJ and HRC (2005).

12 These points are made by Bradbury (1999). He draws insights from ACORD staff, including a presentation by Chris Dolan at a peace research conference in Gulu in September 1999.

13 Crazzolara (1950, 1951 and 1954); Onyango-ku-Odongo and Webster (1976). See also Atkinson (1994). For critical discussion of this literature, see Wrigley (1981); Tim Allen (1991c).

14 *New Vision*, 17 January 2005.

15 No explanation is given in *New Vision* of how this date was established. Some oral historians working in Uganda have attempted to create chronologies based on lists of chiefs, allocating a certain number of years for each succession said to be of a son and adjusting the allocation if there are stories about a brother or older relative succeeding. See, for example, Ogot (1967), and Onyango-ku-Odongo and Webster (1976). The approach has been much criticized. Among other things it underestimates the degree to which stories about the past are myths, associated with ancestor veneration, which provide interpretations of the present.

16 It was not a happy marriage. She accused Olia of being sexually impotent. He responded by murdering her and then killing himself.

17 Bere (1946).

18 As independence approached there was also an eagerness among some Acholi political activists to establish a paramount chief in order to lever concessions from the British and counter the influence of Buganda.

19 Allen (1989, 1991a, 2000); Behrend (1999: 120–21).

20 Liu Institute for Global Studies, 'Northern Uganda – human security update, pursuing peace and justice: international and local initiatives', May 2005.

21 Evans-Pritchard (1940).

Notes

22 See, for example, James (1988). James uses the concept of a cultural archive to describe and analyse this process.

23 In Mozambique, for example, new forms of ritual have emerged which help communities cohere around a collective decision to set aside the past, and see the future through the eyes of young children. See Gibbs (1997).

24 This point is made by Caritas in a recent report (2005: 12).

25 Erin Baines, 'response to the draft report "War and justice in northern Uganda: an assessment of the International Criminal Court's intervention", by Tim Allen, LSE, February 2005', short report distributed by e-mail, Liu Institute for Global Studies, University of British Columbia, 2005, no. 3 <erin.baines@ubc.ca>.

26 Personal communication, 7 February 2005. Sverker Finnstrom presents a fascinating discussion of Acholi rituals in Finnstrom (2003: ch. 7).

27 'Northern Uganda – human security update', op. cit., p. 10.

28 He might also have added that in the past *mato oput* usually required the clan of the wrongdoer to give a girl to the wronged clan – so that she could produce children to replace the one who was killed.

29 The findings of the Caritas research on local healing also confirm that the role of *mato oput* has been overstated. See Caritas (2005).

30 Allen (1999a).

31 ICTJ and HRC (2005). Respondents could give more than one response.

7 Conclusion: a learning process

1 'LRA get new peace terms', *New Vision*, 5 January 2005. A week later Bigombe revealed that the negotiators had met with the LRA again, and that 'We are progressing well ... A very senior LRA commander called Onen Kamdulu even handed over his three wives to me. Two of Kamdulu's wives are pregnant while the third has a baby. This is a very good gesture of peace' ('Bigombe and LRA meet again', *New Vision*, 12 January 2005). Kamdulu later accepted the amnesty himself.

2 Limitations in Acholi customary land tenure, as well as many other crucial issues, are discussed in Adoko and Levine (2004).

3 MSF-Holland (2004b).

4 On occasion the simmering fury boils over. In Awach sub-county of Gulu district, angry residents flogged the body of an LRA commander whom the UPDF had killed in an ambush. Eyewitnesses said the residents overwhelmed UPDF soldiers who tried to stop them ('Mob flogs dead LRA commander', *New Vision*, 22 January 2005).

5 When I returned to Gulu in June 2005 I was confronted by one irate European expatriate aid worker who had read a draft version of parts of this book circulated in February. She clearly felt that it had been a singularly unhelpful contribution. I pointed out that the Paramount Chief himself seemed to have taken on board many of the points. She replied by asserting that that he and others had been forced to go to The Hague and make the conciliatory statements. Apparently serious threats had been made by the Ugandan government. I was alarmed by this information, and took it very seriously, not least because this person was in an influential position as a local legal adviser. It turned out to be untrue, however. The Paramount Chief himself laughed at the suggestion and others who attended the meetings in The Hague have also denied than any such measures were used.

6 'Child protection concerns related to the ICC investigations and possible prosecution of the LRA leadership' <www.redbarnet.dk/Files/Filer/Rapporter/uganda/ICC-Statement_2005.doc>. The statement draws on a draft of parts of this book shared with Save the Children in January.

7 Hovil and Quinn (2005). One of the authors, Joanna Quinn, wrote to me in April, commenting on a draft of this book and agreeing with my analysis of local healing and justice procedures. In her notes she made explicit her view that 'traditional mechanisms of acknowledgement' can play a useful role in post-conflict resolution, but that at this point 'any such mechanisms must be used on a small scale within local communities'.

8 In former Yugoslavia, ending impunity with recourse to international law seems, on balance, to have had positive effects. The indictments of Karadzic and Mladic were linked to their loss of influence and their absence from the Dayton negotiations did not prove very important. There is also some evidence that killing in Kosovo was more limited than it might have been due to fears of possible prosecution, and it has been suggested that the relative absence of reprisals against Bosnian Serbs is connected with the televised images of court proceedings from The Hague (Robertson 2000: 339).

9 I have inverted the meaning of a sentence from Branch (2004: 5), quoted at the end of Chapter 1.

8 Postscript: the warrants

1 'Uganda: ICC issues arrest warrants for LRA leaders', 7 October 2005, IRIN News, UNOCHA <http://www.irinnews.org/report.asp?ReportID=49420&SelectRegion=East_Africa&SelectCountry=UGANDA>.

2 'Decision on the Prosecutor's application for unsealing of the

warrants of arrest', ICC Pe-Trial Chamber II, The Hague, 13 October 2005.

3 'Uganda: first ever arrest warrants by International Criminal Court – a first step towards addressing impunity', Amnesty International Media Briefing, AFR 59/008/2005 (Public), News Service No. 274, 14 October 2005 <http://www.amnestyusa.org/icc/document. do?id=ENGAFR590082005>.

4 This was reported in the Uganda's state-owned New Vision newspaper on Monday 3 October and also picked up by international news services: 'Kony arrest warrant out', *New Vision*, 3 October 2005; Nick Wadhams, 'World court issues first arrest warrants', 7 October 2005 *Guardian Unlimited* <http://216.239.59.104/search?q=cache: TkRHXHj4wtYJ:www.guardian.co.uk/worldlatest/story/0,1280,-5326890,00.html+Ibrahim+Gambari+ICC+warrants&hl=en>.

5 'Warrant of arrest unsealed against five LRA Commanders', ICC press release, The Hague, 14 October 2005, ICC-20051014-110-En <http://www.icc-cpi.int/press/pressreleases/114.html>; ICC pre-trial chamber II, Situation in Uganda Case 01/05, public document, 'Decision on the Prosecutor's application for unsealing of the warrants of arrest', 13 October, 2005.

6 ICC pre-trial chamber II, 'Warrant of arrest for Joseph Kony'; 'Warrant of arrest for Vincent Otti'; 'Warrant of arrest for Dominic Ongwen'; 'Warrant of arrest for Okot Odhiambo'; 'Warrant of arrest for Raska Lukwiya'. All issued on 8 July 2005. The warrant for Joseph Kony was as amended on 27 September 2005. All warrants are available online in redacted version at the ICC's website <http://www.icc-cpi. int/home.html>.

7 'Statement by the Chief Prosecutor on the Uganda arrest warrants', ICC, The Hague, 14 October 2005.

8 'Annan hails International Criminal Court's arrest warrants for five Ugandan rebels', UN News Centre, 14 October 2005 <http://www. un.org/apps/news/story.asp?NewsID=16243&Cr=uganda&Cr1>; UGANDA: 'Indictment of LRA leaders draws widespread praise', UN Office for the Coordination of Humanitarian Affairs, 17 October 2005 <http://www.globalsecurity.org/military/library/news/2005/10/mil-051017-irino4.htm>.

9 'ICC takes decisive step for justice in Uganda, Human Rights Watch', October 2005 <http://hrw.org/english/docs/2005/10/14/uganda11880.htm>; 'Uprooted and forgotten: impunity and human rights in northern Uganda, September 2005' <http://hrw.org/reports/2005/uganda0905/>.

10 'Uganda: first ever arrest warrants by International Criminal

Court – a first step towards addressing impunity', Amnesty International Media Briefing, AFR 59/008/2005 (Public), News Service No. 274, 14 October 2005 <http://www.amnestyusa.org/icc/document.do?id=ENGAFR590082005>.

11 One of many articles presenting critical responses to the warrants is: ICC charges "hinder relief agency efforts" in north Uganda', *Financial Times*, November 2005.

12 'Uganda: ICC issues arrest warrants for LRA leaders', IRIN news, UN OCHA, 7 October 2005 <http://www.irinnews.org/report.asp?ReportID=49420&SelectRegion=East_Africa&SelectCountry=UGANDA>.

13 Branch (2005).

14 'LRA indictees eligible for Uganda's amnesty', 11 October 2005, *Sunday Times*, South Africa. <http://www.suntimes.co.za/zones/sundaytimesNEW/basket6st/basket6st1129007081.aspx>.

15 Allen and Schomerus (2005).

16 Attempts have been made to make a legal argument through parliament that ratification of the Rome Statute is unconstitutional under Ugandan law, but it has been effectively shelved due to government opposition.

17 Walter Ocola commented that: 'Myself I have spent a lot of money by sending airtime to Otti whenever he expresses interest in talks but he turns around and uses the same airtime to coordinate ambushes on innocent people.' 'Northern Uganda leaders scoff at LRA peace deal', UGPulse.com, 6 December 2005 <http://www.ugpulse.com/articles/daily/homepage.asp?ID=209>.

18 The fact that Otti has been talking on a satellite phone to several people, and also that some of his phone calls have been quite long, raises two interesting questions, to which I have been unable to find satisfactory answers. First, who is paying his phone bill? Sometimes he has terminated calls or not answered, apparently because he does not have any more airtime, but then he seems to be given more. Walter Ocola and other peace negotiators have in the past sent Otti airtime for an ordinary mobile phone, but providing airtime for a satellite phone is more complicated and more expensive. Second, why is it not possible to pinpoint Otti's position and either arrest him or kill him? Security experts have explained to me that this can be difficult with an ordinary mobile phone, but it should be relatively easy with a satellite phone.

19 A recent Human Right Watch briefing states that: 'The Ugandan government should reverse its ban on speech and demonstrations linked to the trail of the main opposition candidate for president, Dr. Kizza Besigye, and end its intimidation of the courts ...' Human Rights Watch, 'Uganda: political repression accelerates: US should cut

relations with government forces who stormed courthouse', 23 November 2005 <http://www.hrw.org/english/docs/2005/11/24/uganda12089.htm>.

20 'ICC takes decisive step for justice in Uganda', Human Rights Watch, October 2005 <http://hrw.org/english/docs/2005/10/14/uganda11880.htm>; 'Uprooted and forgotten: impunity and human rights in northern Uganda, September 2005' <http://hrw.org/reports/2005/uganda0905/>.

21 One informant has told me that, on an ad hoc basis, Sudanese officials are increasingly willing to assist the ICC in the investigations of the LRA.

22 Among other things, he has indicated that the OTP is not intending to prepare further warrants for LRA commanders, unless they relate to new crimes. In so doing he has implied that those LRA commanders who have surrendered and accepted the amnesty do not need to fear prosecution.

23 'Decision to convene a status report conference on matters related to safety and security in Uganda', pre-trial chamber II, ICC, The Hague, 25 November 2005.

24 'Decision to convene a status conference on the investigation in the situation in Uganda in relation to the application of Article 53', pre-trial chamber II, ICC, The Hague, 2 December 2005.

25 Pressure have been mounting for the Security Council to pass a resolution on northern Uganda for some time. Resolution 1460 of 2003 dealt with the involvement of children in armed conflict, and in places suggests specific reference to northern Uganda, without actually mentioning it. In April 2005, the Security Council President made a press statement in response to a briefing on the situation by Jan Egeland. Council members 'strongly condemned the appalling atrocities carried out by the so-called Lord's Resistance Army ...' They also 'called on the Government of Uganda to enhance its protection for displaced persons and those providing essential services to them ...' 'Press statement on northern Uganda by Security Council President', UN Security Council, SC/8057 AFR/900 <http://www.un.org/News/Press/docs/2004/sc8057.doc.htm>. International aid agencies, however, have been lobbying persistently for more decisive action: 'Uganda: Security Council urged to intervene in northern war', IRIN News, 10 May 2005 <http://www.globalsecurity.org/military/library/news/2005/05/mil-050510-irin01.htm>; 'UN Security Council must act to protect civilians in northern Uganda as conflict kills 1,000 people every week', Oxfam Press Release, 9 November 2005 <http://www.oxfam.org/en/news/pressreleases/2005/pr051109_uganda>. The 'Gulu Walk' movement has been another

source of pressure. A recent briefing has noted that: 'In December, the United Kingdom of Great Britain and Northern Ireland hold the Presidency of the UN Security Council and have already made it clear that northern Uganda is a priority. During a visit to Gulu last week, British High Commissioner Francois Gordon said that, "Nineteen years of war characterised by abductions, rape, slavery of children and all sorts of humiliation of civilians is too much for the people ... Kony and his LRA rebellion in northern Uganda will later this month be tabled for discussion before the UN Security Council" ...' Gulu Walk, 19 December 2005 <http://www.guluwalk.com/news/>.

26 For an interesting recent discussion of the Bush administration's policy towards the ICC, see 'Hunting Kony: will the ICC's first indictments inspire détente between the Bush administration and the World Court?', *American Prospect*, 7 October 2005 <http://www.prospect.org/web/page.ww?section=root&name=ViewWeb&articleId=10392>.

27 As this book goes to press in January 2006, pressures on the ICC are intensifying. In particular, Chief Prosecutor Mareno-Ocampo is being criticized for not having delivered suspects for trial, although it is hard to see what he could have done about it. The ICC judges are also keeping a tight rein over his office. Tensions within the court are said not to be helped by rumours that the OTP had something to do with the leaks about the sealed warrants in September 2005. Meanwhile, the LRA continues to operate on both sides of the Uganda-Sudan border, and Vincent Otti has said that he will now continue fighting until after the Ugandan presidential elections. There are allegations that the LRA is still receiving supplies from factions associated with the Sudan government. The SPLA have indicated that they will support negotiations, but SPLA officials claim that no discussions with the LRA have actually occurred, and there are reports of the SPLA preparing for an offensive against LRA groups operating to the west of Juba, around Maridi. Joseph Kony himself is keeping a low profile, but is said to be operating with an LRA group to the northeast of Juba (i.e. over a hundred miles from the Uganda border).

Bibliography

Adoko, J. and S. Levine (2004) *Land Matters in Displacement: The Importance of Land Rights in Acholiland and What Threatens Them*, Kampala: CSOPNU, December <csopnu@yahoo.com>

Afako, B. (2004) *International and National Challenges to the Amnesty Process in Uganda*, mimeo, February

Akuma, C. O., I. Amony and G. Otim (2005) *Suffering in Silence: A Study of Sexual and Gender Based Violence in Pabbo Camp, Gulu District, Northern Uganda*, Gulu: Gulu District Sub Working Group on SGBV

Allen, T. (1989) 'Violence and moral knowledge', *Cambridge Anthropology*, 13(2): 45–66

— (1991a) 'The quest for therapy in Moyo District', in M. Twaddle and H. B. Hansen (eds), *Changing Uganda: Dilemmas of Structural Adjustment and Revolutionary Change*, London: James Currey, pp. 149–61

— (1991b) 'Understanding Alice: Uganda's Holy Spirit Movement in context', *Africa*, 61(3): 370–99

— (1991c) 'Histories and contexts: using pasts in the present on the Sudan/Uganda border', in P. Baxter and R. Fardon (eds), *Texts in Action*, Bulletin of the John Rylands Library University Library of Manchester, 73(3), autumn

— (1992) 'Upheaval, affliction and health: a Ugandan case study', in H. Bernstein, B. Crow and H. Johnson (eds), *Rural Livelihoods: Crises and Responses*, Oxford: Oxford University Press

— (1999a) 'The violence of healing', *Sociologus*, 47(2): 101–28

— (1999b) 'Perceiving contemporary wars', in T. Allen and J. Seaton (eds), *The Media of Conflict*, London: Zed Books

— (2000) 'Understanding health: biomedicine and local knowledge in northern Uganda', in R. Edmondson and C. Kelleher (eds), *Health Promotion: New Discipline or Multi-discipline?*, Dublin: Irish Academic Press

— (2006) 'AIDS and evidence: interrogating some Ugandan myths', *Journal of Biosocial Science*, 38(1)

Allen, T. and S. Heald (2004) 'HIV/AIDS policy in Africa: what has worked in Uganda and what has failed in Botswana?', *Journal of International Development*, 16: 1141–54

Allen, T. and M. Schomerus (2005) *A Hard Homecoming: Lessons Learned from the Reception Center Process on Effective Interventions for Former 'Abductees' in Northern Uganda*, study commissioned by UNICEF and USAID, Kampala, December

Atkinson, R. A. (1994) *The Roots of Ethnicity: The Origins of the Acholi of Uganda before 1800*, Philadelphia: University of Pennsylvania Press

Bayart, J. F., S. Ellis and B. Hibou (1999) *The Criminalization of the African State*, Bloomington: Indiana University Press

Behrend, H. (1999) *Alice Lakwena and the Holy Spirits*, Oxford: James Currey

Bere, R. M. (1946) 'Awich – a biographical note and a chapter of Acholi history', *Uganda Journal*, 10(2): 76–8

Bradbury, M. (1999) *Reflecting on Peace Practice: An Overview of Initiatives for Peace in Acholi, Northern Uganda*, Paper commissioned by the Collaborative for Development Action, Inc., October

Branch, A. (2004) 'International justice, local injustice: the International Criminal Court in northern Uganda', *Dissent*, summer

— (2005) 'The International Criminal Court in northern Uganda: a legal, political and moral critique', unpublished paper, December

Caritas (2005) 'Traditional ways of preventing and solving conflicts in Acholi', Psychosocial Support Programme, Gulu Archdiocese, January

Ciantia, F. (2004) 'HIV seroprevalence in northern Uganda: the complex relationship between AIDS and conflict', *Journal of Medicine and the Person*, 2(4): 172–5

Citizens for Global Solutions (2004) *In Uncharted Waters: Seeking Justice before the Atrocities Have Stopped – the International Criminal Court in Uganda and the Democratic Republic of the Congo* <www.global solutions.org>, June

Crazzolara, J. P. (1950, 1951 and 1954) *The Lwoo Part I: Lwoo Migrations*; *The Lwoo Part II: Lwoo Traditions*; and *The Lwoo Part III: Lwoo Clans*, Verona: Museum Combonianum/Instituto missioni africane

CSOPNU (2005) *The International Criminal Court Investigation in Northern Uganda*, Briefing paper, 1 February <csopnu@yahoo.com>

Des Forges, A. and T. Longman (2004) 'Legal responses to genocide in Rwanda', in E. Stover and H. M. Weinstein (eds), *My Neighbour, My Enemy: Justice and Community in the Aftermath of Mass Atrocity*, Cambridge: Cambridge University Press

De Temmerman, E. (2001) *Aboke Girls: Children Abducted in Northern Uganda*, Kampala: Fountain Publishers

De Waal, A. (1997) *Famine Crimes*, Oxford: James Currey

Dolan, C. (2002) 'Which children count? The politics of children's rights in northern Uganda', in O. Lucima (ed.), *Protracted Conflict, Elusive Peace*, London: ACCORD, Conciliation Resources <www. c-r.org/accord/uganda/accord11/acknow.shtml>

— (2005) *Understanding War and Its Continuation: The Case of Northern Uganda*, London: Development Studies Institute, London School of Economics

Dolan, C. and E. Bagenda (2004) *Militarisation and Its Impacts*, February, available from <Chris.Dolan@dial.pipex.com>

Doom, R. and K. Vlassenroot (1999) 'Kony's message: a new Koine? The Lord's Resistance Army in northern Uganda', *African Affairs*, 98: 5–36

Duffield, M. (2001) *Global Governance and the New Wars: The Merging of Development and Security*, London: Zed Books

Evans-Pritchard, E. E. (1937) *Witchcraft, Oracles, and Magic among the Azande*, Oxford: Clarendon Press

— (1940) *The Nuer: A Description of the Modes of Livelihood and Political Institutions of a Nilotic People*, Oxford: Clarendon Press

FAFO (2005) *Northern Uganda IDP Study June 2005*, Institute for Labour and Social Research <fafo@fafo.no>

Falk, L., J. Lenz and P. Okuma (2004) *Sleepless in Gulu: A Study of the Dynamics behind the Child Night Commuting Phenomena in Gulu, Uganda*, Kampala: SCiU, May

Finnstrom, S. (2003) *Living with Bad Surroundings: War and Existential Uncertainty in Acholiland, Northern Uganda*, Uppsala: Uppsala Studies in Cultural Anthropology, no. 35

Fletcher, L. E. and H. M. Weinstein (2004) 'A world unto itself? The application of international justice in former Yugoslavia', in E. Stover and H. M. Weinstein (eds), *My Neighbour, My Enemy: Justice and Community in the Aftermath of Mass Atrocity*, Cambridge: Cambridge University Press

Gersony, R. (1997) *The Anguish of Northern Uganda*, Report submitted to the US embassy, Kampala, and USAID mission, Kampala, August <www.usaid.gov/regions/afr/conflictweb/reports/gersiny/gersony_uganda.pdf>

Gibbs, S. (1997) 'Postwar social reconstruction in Mozambique: reframing children's experiences on trauma and healing', in K. Kumar (ed.), *Rebuilding Societies after Civil War: Critical Role for International Assistance*, London: Lynne Reinner, pp. 227–38

Girling, F. (1960) *The Acholi of Uganda*, London: HMSO

Harrell-Bond, B. (1986) *Imposing Aid*, Oxford: Oxford University Press

Heald, S. (1989) *Controlling Anger: The Sociology of Gisu Violence*, Manchester: Manchester University Press

Higgins, R. (1994) *Problems and Process: International Law and How We Use It*, Oxford: Clarendon Press

Hovil, L. and J. R. Quinn (2005) *Peace First, Justice Later: Traditional Justice in Northern Uganda*, Refugee Law Project Working Paper no.17, July <www.research@refugeelawproject.org>

ICTJ and HRC (2005) *Forgotten Voices: A Population-based Survey on Attitudes about Peace and Justice in Northern Uganda*, International Center for Transitional Justice and Human Rights Center, University of California, July

James, W. (1988) *The Listening Ebony: Moral Knowledge, Religion and Power among the Uduk of Sudan*, Oxford: Clarendon Press

Jia, B. B. (1999) 'The differing concepts of war crimes and crimes against humanity in international law', in G. S. Goodwin-Gill and S. Talmon (eds), *The Reality of International Law*, Oxford: Clarendon Press

Johnson, D. H. (2003) *The Root Causes of Sudan's Civil Wars*, Oxford: James Currey

Kaldor, M. (1999) *New Wars and Old Wars: Organised Violence in a Global Era*, Cambridge: Polity Press

Keen, D. (1994) *The Benefits of Famine*, Princeton, NJ: Princeton University Press

Lomo, Z. and L. Hovil (2004) *Behind the Violence: Causes, Consequences and the Search for Solutions to the War in Northern Uganda*, Kampala: Refugee Law Project Working Paper no. 11, February <www.refugeelawproject.org/working%20papers/RLP%20WP11%20-Northern%20Uganda.pdf>

Lucima, O. (ed.) (2002) *Protracted Conflict, Elusive Peace: Initiatives to End the Violence in Northern Uganda*, London: ACCORD, Conciliation Resources, <www.c-r.org/accord/uganda/accord11/index.shtml>

McKay, S. and D. Mazurana (2004) *Where are the Girls?: Girls in the Fighting Forces in Northern Uganda, Sierra Leone and Mozambique: Their Lives During and After the War*, Montreal: Rights and Democracy

MSF-Holland (2004a) *Internally Displaced Camps in Lira and Pader, Northern Uganda: A Baseline Survey, Preliminary Report*, Uganda: MSF-Holland, November

— (2004b) *Pader: A Community in Crisis: A Preliminary Analysis of MSF-Holland's Baseline Mental Health Assessment in Pader*, Uganda: MSF-Holland, October

Nyeko, B. and O. Lucima (2002) 'Profiles of the parties to the conflict', in O. Lucima (ed.), *Protracted Conflict, Elusive Peace*, London: ACCORD, Conciliation Resources <www.c-r.org/accord/uganda/accord11>

Ogot, B. (1967) *History of the Southern Luo*, Nairobi: East African Publishing House

Onyango-ku-Odongo and J. B.Webster (eds) (1976) *The Central Lwo During the Aconya*, Nairobi: East Africa Literature Bureau

Pain, D. (1997) *The Bending of the Spears: Producing Consensus for Peace & Development in Northern Uganda*, London: International Alert and *Kacoke Madit* <www.km-net.org/publications/spear.doc>.

p'Bitek, O. (1971) *Religion of the Central Luo*, Nairobi: East Africa Literature Bureau

Refugee Law Project (2004) *Position Paper on the ICC*, Makerere: Faculty of Law, Makerere University <www.refugeelawproject.org>

Reiff, D. (2002) *A Bed for the Night: Humanitarianism in Crisis*, New York: Simon & Schuster

Robertson, G. (2000) *Crimes against Humanity: The Struggle for Global Justice*, new edn, London: Penguin

Sands, P. (2005) *Lawless World: America and the Making and Breaking of Global Rules*, London: Penguin

Schlenker, R. (1999) *Witchcraft and the Legitimation of the State in Uganda*, MA dissertation, School of Oriental and African Studies, University of London, October

SciU (2004a) *Record of ICC Discussion Meeting, Acholi Inn, Gulu, Friday 13th August 2004*, Mimeo, Gulu: SciU

— (2004b) *SciU Statement on ICC Prosecution of LRA*, Kampala: SCiU, February

Stover, E. and H. M. Weinstein (2004), 'Introduction: conflict, justice and reclamation', in E. Stover and H. M. Weinstein (eds), *My Neighbour, My Enemy: Justice and Community in the Aftermath of Mass Atrocity*, Cambridge: Cambridge University Press

UNICEF (2001) *Abductions in Northern Uganda and South-western Uganda: 1986–2001*, Uganda: UNICEF, November

Van Acket, F. (2004) 'Uganda and the Lord's Resistance Army: the new order no one ordered', *African Affairs*, 103(412): 335–57

WHO (2005) *Health and Mortality Survey among Internally Displaced Persons in Gulu, Kitgum and Pader Districts, Northern Uganda*, Republic of Uganda: Ministry of Health, July

World Vision (2004) *Pawns of Politics: Children, Conflict and Peace in Northern Uganda*, Washington, DC: World Vision

Wrigley, C. C. (1981) 'The problem of the Lwo', *History of Africa*, 8: 119–245

Index

Index

African Arguments

ZED BOOKS IN ASSOCIATION WITH THE INTERNATIONAL AFRICAN INSTITUTE

African Arguments is a series of short books about Africa today. Aimed at the growing number of students and general readers who want to know more about the continent, these books intend to highlight many of the longer-term strategic as well as immediate political issues confronting the African continent. They will get to the heart of why Africa is the way it is and how it is changing. The books are scholarly but engaged, substantive as well as topical.

Titles already published

Julie Flint and Alex de Waal, *Darfur: A Short History of a Long War*
Tim Allen, *Trial Justice: The International Criminal Court and the Lord's Resistance Army*

Titles in preparation

Alex de Waal, *AIDS and Power: Why There is No Political Crisis – Yet*
Tajudeen Abdul-Raheem, *The African Union: False Start or New Dawn?*
Richard Dowden and Simon Maxwell, *Aid to Africa: Help or Hindrance?*

Published by Zed Books and the IAI with the support of the following organizations:

Global Equity Initiative The Global Equity Initiative seeks to advance our understanding and tackle the challenges of globally inequitable development. Located at Harvard University, it has international collaborative research programmes on security, health, capabilities and philanthropy.

InterAfrica Group The InterAfrica Group is the regional centre for dialogue on issues of development, democracy, conflict resolution and humanitarianism in the Horn of Africa. It was founded in 1988 and is based in Addis Ababa, and has programmes supporting democracy in Ethiopia and partnership with the African Union and IGAD. <www.sas. upenn.edu/African_Studies/ Hornet/menu_Intr_Afr.html>

International African Institute The International African Institute's principal aim is to promote scholarly understanding of Africa, notably its changing societies, cultures and languages. Founded in 1926 and based in London, it supports a range of seminars and publications including the journal *Africa*. <www.iaionthe.net>

Justice Africa Justice Africa initiates and supports African civil society activities in support of peace, justice and democracy in Africa. Founded in 1999, it has a range of activities relating to peace in the Horn of Africa, HIV/AIDS and democracy, and the African Union. <www.justiceafrica.org>

Royal African Society Now more than a hundred years old, the Royal African Society today is Britain's leading organization promoting Africa's cause. Through its journal, *African Affairs*, and by organizing meetings, discussions and other activities, the society strengthens links between Africa and

Britain and encourages understanding of Africa and its relations with the rest of the world. <www.royalafricansociety.org>

Social Science Research Council The Social Science Research Council brings much needed expert knowledge to public issues. Founded in 1923 and based in New York, it brings together researchers, practitioners and policy-makers in every continent. <www.ssrc.org>